THEODORE ROOSEVELT

THEODORE ROOSEVELT

★ ★ ★ ★ ★ ★ ★

CHAMPION OF THE AMERICAN SPIRIT

BY BETSY HARVEY KRAFT

CLARION BOOKS

NEW YORK

Few books are the work of the author only. In writing this book I was fortunate enough to have the thoughtful guidance of editor Virginia Buckley and the careful attention to detail and design from other staff members at Clarion. Wallace Dailey, curator of the Theodore Roosevelt Collection at Harvard University, gave extraordinary help in providing photographs and manuscript images. Linda Milano, assistant director of the Theodore Roosevelt Association, generously offered insights and information not available from other sources. Thanks to all.

Clarion Books
a Houghton Mifflin Company imprint
215 Park Avenue South, New York, NY 10003
Copyright © 2003 by Betsy Harvey Kraft

Photograph credits:
Theodore Roosevelt Collection: Harvard College Library. By permission of Houghton Library, Harvard University: pages i, xii, 2, 4, 6, 7, 9, 10, 12, 16 (right), 23, 28, 30, 44, 49, 51, 58, 59, 64, 66, 68, 71, 78, 89 (middle and bottom), 90, 92, 113, 123, 125, 129, 138, 142, 144, 145, 150.
Library of Congress: pages ii, viii, 16 (left), 21, 34, 42, 46, 52, 56, 63, 73, 77, 82, 83, 86, 88, 89 (top), 95, 96, 99, 103, 107, 109, 111, 112, 115, 118, 120, 126, 133, 139, 140, 143, 146, 148, 152, 155, 156, 157, 160, 162.
U.S. Naval Historical Center: page 134.

The text was set in 13-point Goudy Old Style.

For information about permission to reproduce selections from this book, write to Permissions, Houghton Mifflin Company, 215 Park Avenue South, New York, NY 10003.

www.houghtonmifflinbooks.com

Printed in the U.S.A.

Library of Congress Cataloging-in-Publication Data

Kraft, Betsy Harvey.
Theodore Roosevelt : champion of the American spirit / by Betsy Harvey Kraft.
p.   cm.
Summary: A biography of the energetic New Yorker who became the twenty-sixth president of the United States and who once exclaimed, "No one has ever enjoyed life more than I have."
ISBN 0-618-14264-9 (alk. paper)
1. Roosevelt, Theodore, 1858–1919—Juvenile literature. 2. Presidents—United States—Biography—Juvenile literature. [1. Roosevelt, Theodore, 1858–1919. 2. Presidents.] I. Title.
E757 .K73 2003
973.91'1'092—dc21   2002152825

VB 10 9 8 7 6 5 4 3 2 1

For Kate

Contents

Theodore Roosevelt, a great believer of "the strenuous life," brought new energy and style to the presidency. He once chopped down a tree with such vigor that an observer "felt sorry for the tree." Roosevelt liked almost all outdoor sports except sailing, fearing he might become becalmed.

"THE STRENUOUS LIFE"

As he rode up the driveway to the governor's mansion in Albany, New York, Gifford Pinchot, head of the nation's forest services, was greeted by a strange scene. Leaning out the second-story window was a red-faced gentleman, who was lowering a rope with a small child at the other end. The man's eyeglasses glinted in the sunlight. His boyish grin revealed an even set of large white teeth as he yelled encouragement in a high-pitched, exuberant voice. He lowered other children, then came to greet his guest. His six lively offspring, he explained, needed to learn how to escape from an upstairs window in case of fire, and he had invented a game in which they were fleeing from an imaginary band of savages.

The man in the glasses was Theodore Roosevelt, the forty-two-year-old governor of New York. Within months, he would be the twenty-sixth president of the United States.

The scene was typical of Roosevelt. He never lost his enthusiasm for behaving like a boy. "You must remember, the president is about six," a friend once said of him. He sometimes stopped in the middle of serious national business to romp with his children. He wanted them to share his enthusiasm for "the strenuous life," leaving no minute of the day unfilled.

Visitors had to take part in the strenuous life, too. Pinchot had barely said hello before the governor challenged him to a boxing match. Roosevelt was a good boxer, and he was always "dee-lighted" (one of his favorite words) when he beat

☆ ix

an opponent. Later, the two sat down to talk about one of their mutual passions—conserving the environment.

"Look!" Roosevelt might have pointed out. "There's a sharp-tailed sparrow." Or he might have said, "Listen. That's the song of a wood thrush." Theodore Roosevelt was familiar with every kind of bird in the state of New York. And his knowledge of nature went beyond bird watching. Pinchot was the country's leading expert on forests and knew more than most people about trees, plants, and animals. But Theodore Roosevelt knew as much as he did or even more.

Roosevelt was a serious student of the outdoors. He could identify dozens of birds simply by their songs. He recognized their coloring, their habitat, and their mating habits. He had encountered firsthand the animals of the American West: bison, antelope, wolves, and bears. He was, in fact, one of the world's leading experts on mammals. He could easily have become a professional natural scientist. Instead, he chose politics.

Roosevelt was like a carefree boy when he was playing with his children, but he was dead serious about politics. Politics gave him the power to act, to change things for the better. Politics called for men of action, men willing to fight. And Theodore Roosevelt loved a good fight.

No one would have thought that the small, frail baby born on October 27, 1858, would grow up to be a fighter. He was pale and delicate, and his family worried that he might not make it past his fourth birthday. He did, though, and for sixty years he filled every waking moment with unbounded enthusiasm for life. Complex and tireless, he was a patchwork of contradictions. Born into a family of wealthy aristocrats, he was as comfortable with the rough-and-tumble cowboys of the American West as with sophisticated New Yorkers. He read and wrote voraciously, but he never sat still for long. He loved rigorous hikes through the woods, endless games of tennis, and long rows across Long Island Sound, near where he lived for much of his life.

He negotiated peace between warring nations, yet he was one of America's most enthusiastic soldiers. He relished hunting and shooting, but he was a leader in preserving America's natural resources.

He doted on his wife and six children and thought it was an American duty to have large families. Yet he thought nothing of spending weeks away from home, leaving his wife with the job of corralling their obstreperous tribe. He loved to laugh, but he suffered personal tragedies and setbacks that left him solitary and depressed.

He never stayed down for long, however. Theodore Roosevelt plunged into life, pulling his family, his friends, and his nation along with him. "No one," he once exclaimed, "has ever enjoyed life more than I have."

At seven, Theodore Roosevelt (called "Teedie") was frail and suffered from asthma, but he rode horses, swam, hiked, and collected animals and birds for his "Roosevelt Museum of Natural History."

Chapter 1

"THE SWEETNESS OF HOME"

Teedie was four, and he had just bitten his sister on the arm. In terror he fled to the kitchen, grabbed a handful of raw dough, and darted under a table. Maybe the cook would save him from his father's wrath. But when Theodore Roosevelt Sr. strode in minutes later, he immediately dropped to his knees and reached for his son. In desperation, Teedie stood up, hurled the dough at his father, and headed for the stairs. But his father was quick, and Teedie was only halfway up the steps before he was captured. Although Father was kind and loving, he made it clear that there would be no more biting.

Father was the most important person in the house on East Twentieth Street. When he came home in the evenings from his office at the family importing business and his work with various charities, the Roosevelt children gathered in his bedroom. They looked on, fascinated, as he removed his gold watch and other treasures from his pockets. Then they scrambled downstairs, pushing one another aside to claim the coveted seat next to him on the sofa.

The neighborhood where the Roosevelts lived in New York City was more like a large, overgrown town than a city. Teedie could jump down the front steps of the family townhouse and run next door to Uncle Robert's house. His aunt kept animals in the backyard: peacocks, parrots, pheasants, a monkey, and even for a short time, a cow.

At home there was Father's library, full of serious books bound in leather.

☆ 1

Edith Carow was a childhood friend of Teedie's sister Corinne. Years later his sister Anna (Bamie) arranged an "accidental" meeting between the two.

Sometimes, when Teedie wanted to be away from the constant buzz of the household, he would lug a giant illustrated book about wild African animals into the living room and try to puzzle out the words under the pictures. Or, if he wanted company, there was always Anna, his older sister, nicknamed Bamie. And he could play with his brother, Elliott, and his younger sister, Corinne.

Or he might walk a few blocks south to visit his grandparents at their elegant brownstone on Union Square. Sometimes he and Corinne walked to Edith Carow's. Edith was Corinne's friend, but she liked Teedie, too, and together the three of them spent long afternoons playing house or listening to stories Teedie made up.

One April day in 1865, Edith and Corinne went to visit Grandfather Roosevelt's house. Teedie was there and so was Elliott. Why were the lampposts draped in black, Edith wondered, and why were the people in the streets crying? Civil War veterans, some without legs or arms, others on crutches, stood in front of the house. She was terrified, and Teedie and Elliott decided that she was a crybaby and locked her in a closet. Then the boys went upstairs, leaned out a window, and watched the funeral procession for Abraham Lincoln, the assassinated president of the United States, pass solemnly in front of the house.

Teedie knew that Mother and Father had disagreed about President Lincoln and the Civil War. Mother was a beautiful Georgia belle, and her mother and her sister, Anna, lived with the Roosevelt family in New York. Grandmother Bulloch entertained the children with stories of life on the Georgia plantation they had left behind, and Aunt Anna taught them their lessons when they were young. The three women sided with the South and the people they knew there. Mother's two brothers, Uncle Jimmie and Uncle Irvine, had served in the Confederate navy.

Teedie's father could have fought for the North. He was young and physically fit and probably could have been an officer in the Union army. But he did not want to upset his wife. She would not have tolerated her husband fighting against her friends and family from the South.

Theodore Roosevelt Sr. did not go to war. Instead, like many wealthy men of his time, he hired someone to fight in his place. Then he traveled to Union military camps to urge Northern soldiers to send part of their paychecks back to their wives and children rather than spend it on cheap liquor. It was typical of him to try to do something for people in need.

Teedie's grandfather and great-grandfather had built a family fortune by importing glass and owning real estate in New York City. His father did not have to work and easily could have spent his days dining at exclusive clubs or riding horseback. Instead, he devoted his time to improving the lives of New York's less fortunate. He volunteered regularly at the Newsboys' Lodging House, which provided a refuge and education for homeless boys. He often took his own children along to help. He raised money for a hospital for children with physical disabilities and helped establish the Children's Aid Society. With several of his wealthy friends, he founded the American Museum of Natural History and the Metropolitan Museum of Art, providing New York City with two cultural institutions open to the public.

Teedie's father also spent a lot of time taking care of his oldest son. By the time he was three years old, Teedie was seized with terrifying bouts of asthma, which left him struggling for breath. All during Teedie's childhood, Theodore Sr. and his wife, Mittie, tried every known remedy of the times. He poured brandy down his son's throat and took him for midnight carriage rides through the streets of New York City in hopes that the fresh air would clear his lungs. Once Teedie had to smoke a

Six-year-old Teedie and his brother, Elliott *(tiny figures in shuttered window at upper left)*, watch President Lincoln's funeral procession from their grandfather's flag-draped townhouse in New York City. The two brothers locked Edith Carow in a closet when she became frightened and began to cry.

cigar—the doctor thought it would help, but it didn't. The circles around the young boy's eyes grew darker. He had to sleep propped upright on a pile of pillows.

During the day, though, Teedie was usually out exploring the neighborhood. One morning, when he was seven, his mother sent him to the market for strawberries, and he made a wonderful discovery. There on the sidewalk, lying on a wooden slab outside a fish market, was a dead seal. He was fascinated and wanted to know more. How long was it? How much did it weigh? How many inches around was its skull? He got a folding ruler from home and inched it around the decaying carcass, making notes as he went. The measurements, Roosevelt wrote years later, "were totally meaningless." But at the time the seal filled him with "every possible feeling of romance and adventure."

This was the beginning of Teedie's "Roosevelt Museum of Natural History." Besides the seal's skull, there were birds' nests, shells, insects, mice, and an occasional snake. When the collection became too big for his bedroom, he moved it into the upstairs hallway. When it outgrew the hallway, he moved it to the attic.

Any animal, alive or dead, captured Teedie's attention. The Roosevelt house became home to snakes kept in water pitchers and a snapping turtle tied to a tub in the laundry room. His mother threw out six dead mice after she found them in the icebox. ("A great loss to science," Teedie lamented in his journal.) Once he caused a mild panic on a city bus when he tipped his hat to an acquaintance and a live frog leaped from on top of his head into the crowd of passengers.

Teedie was never afraid of animals, but his asthma made him physically weak. All his heroes were strong men: men like his father, bold African game hunters, his uncle Jimmie. He feared that he never could live up to them.

As a pale, timid ten-year-old, Teedie traveled abroad with his family for a grand tour of European countries. During that trip he suffered several serious asthma attacks and was terribly homesick. Still, he was able to take a twenty-mile hike through the Swiss Alps. And to pass the time he had read and kept a journal full of misspelled tales about his adventures. But when their ship sailed into New York Harbor, Teedie was overjoyed to be home. "Hip, hip hooray," he wrote in his journal.

Teedie was happy to be home, but his father continued to worry about his son. When he was eleven, his father sat him down for a serious talk. "Theodore," he told him, "you have the mind, but you have not the body, and without the help of the body the mind cannot go as far as it should. You must *make* your body," he continued. "It is hard drudgery to make one's body, but I know you will do it."

Teedie would do anything to please his father. Besides, he did not like being defenseless. Recently, three boys had ganged up on him during a carriage ride, and Teedie had been too scared and too weak to fight back. It had been a humiliating experience, and he was determined to change. Father helped by outfitting the upstairs porch as a kind of outdoor gym. Methodically, Teedie began a daily fitness workout. He lifted weights. He chinned himself, did pushups, and swung on parallel bars. And he learned to box.

In 1872, when Teedie was fourteen, the entire Roosevelt clan took another trip

Fourteen-year-old Teedie *(far left)* poses dramatically with his brother, Elliott *(second from left)*, sister Corrine *(second from right)*, and two cousins. The group, known as the Dresden Literary American Club, read poems and stories, wrote plays, and adopted the motto "We Are No Asses."

abroad. They visited Egypt, Palestine, Greece, Syria, and later Germany, where the boys and Corinne stayed on to study languages. On the trip to Egypt Teedie was eager to explore. For two months the family cruised up the Nile River in a dahabeah, a slow-moving, comfortably outfitted boat. Earlier, for his fourteenth birthday, Teedie's father had given him a double-barreled, breech-loading gun. After he missed several obvious targets and had trouble seeing the letters on a large billboard, Teedie was diagnosed as being very nearsighted. His first pair of eyeglasses "literally opened an entirely new world to me," he wrote years later.

Now, cruising along the Nile, he was able to see many of the exotic birds along the river's shoreline. After a morning of shooting, he would take his prey back to the boat and use the taxidermy skills he had learned in the States. "I have had great enjoyment from the shooting here," he wrote to his aunt, "as I have procured between one and two hundred skins."

Teedie kept collecting once he was in Germany, where he, his brother, and his younger sister spent several months. Elliott and Teedie lived with one family in Dresden, and Corinne with another; she was terribly homesick. Teedie's hosts were horrified when they discovered that their young guest was practicing taxidermy in his room. "My scientific pursuits cause the family a good deal of consternation," he said in a letter home. "My arsenic was confiscated and my mice thrown (with the tongs) out of the window."

In Dresden, Teedie lived with a German family, filling his room with hedgehogs, snakes, and other animals. In an illustrated letter home he depicts a horrified maid flinging a dead mouse out the window.

A Note About Roosevelt's Many Names

Theodore Roosevelt went by many names throughout his life. When he was a child, his family called him Teedie or Thee. As an adolescent, he preferred Ted. At Harvard close friends and his future wife, Alice Lee, called him Teddy, a name he came to dislike in later years. Many people continued to call him Teddy, but he regarded them as presumptuous and too familiar. When be became president, he preferred Theodore. And he often signed correspondence with a simple "TR." After he left the presidency, he was happy to be called Colonel, a reference to his days as leader of the Rough Riders.

Still, he and Elliott managed to find time to study. They were up at half-past six and studied from seven-thirty till lunchtime. They studied again till ten at night, with breaks for tea and supper. He was "getting on very well" with German, he reported, and could now understand French, which he was also learning, "almost as well as English."

Back in the United States, the Roosevelts had moved uptown into an elegant new mansion on West Fifty-seventh Street, off Fifth Avenue. It was much more formal than the old townhouse on Twentieth Street. But the top floor housed a gymnasium, and Teedie, who now wanted to be called Ted, continued his rigorous exercise routine.

At the family's summer house in Oyster Bay, on Long Island, he spent hours hiking, rowing, riding, and collecting. "Dear Bamie," he wrote to his sister back in New

York City. "At present I am writing in a rather smelly room, as the fresh skins of six night herons are reposing on the table beside me; the said night herons being the product of yesterdays expedition to Loyd's (how do you spell that name?) neck. Elliot and I rowed over there in his little rowboat, although it was pretty rough.... My wretched horse has not yet recovered, but in two or three days I hope to be able to ride him." (Ted often misspelled his brother's name, which annoyed Elliott no end.)

Ted began a sports diary in which he recorded his chest, waist, thigh, neck, and shoulder measurements. At age seventeen he weighed 124 pounds and was five feet eight inches tall. One entry showed that he had run a hundred-yard foot race in thirteen seconds. Another noted that he could do a standing jump of eight feet. He entered Elliott's performance, too—perhaps because his brother had jumped only seven feet three inches.

Ted also started a bird list. At Oyster Bay he spent hours in the woods. He scanned the trees for birds, listened to their songs, and watched where they lived and what they did. Then he wrote down everything he observed. Sometimes he took notes on as many as eighteen birds a day. His lists were very detailed: he recorded the Latin and common name for each bird, its sex, the date he found it, the contents he found in its stomach if he dissected it, its coloring, and the sound of its song.

One of young Teedie's sketches of live animal specimens. He was so nearsighted, the "only things I could study were those I ran against or stumbled over," he remembered in his autobiography. Just before he turned fourteen, he began wearing glasses, which later became a TR trademark.

Maybe, he thought, he would become a professional natural scientist. He could study at Harvard, one of the country's oldest universities, which had fine professors in the natural sciences. He and the other Roosevelt children had always been taught at home, first by Aunt Anna, then by tutors. He had read Shakespeare, poetry, the classics, and books on natural science. He could read and write German and French and had learned history and geography both from books and his travels abroad.

But there were gaps in his formal education. He needed to know Latin, Greek, and mathematics. Father suggested that Ted work with special tutor, who would prepare him in those subjects. For the next year, he studied intensely and passed all eight of the required exams. In the fall of 1876, Ted, now almost eighteen, left New York City for Cambridge, Massachusetts, and became a freshman at Harvard.

Before he enrolled, Bamie, Ted's older sister, found and decorated an apartment in Cambridge for him. What would he have done without her, Ted wrote home. "I do not know whether to admire most the curtains, the paper or the carpet," he said.

After arriving at Harvard College, Theodore writes his older sister, Anna (Bamie), thanking her for decorating his room. He wants his valise, books, towels, and bedding sent "immediately."

He had added his own touches, too: stuffed animals, mounted birds, antlers on the wall, and a birdcage for the occasional resident snake or turtle.

On a typical day a "scout," or servant, polished his boots and lit the fire in the fireplace. Then Ted headed for a breakfast of "biscuits, toast, chops or beef steak, and buckwheat cakes." He had found the food at the commons, where most of the students ate, "highly distasteful" and had arranged to eat with other wealthy young men at a members-only dining club. The rest of the day he was busy with studying, classes, sports, and social activities.

Professors and students were not sure at first what to make of Ted Roosevelt. He seemed to be everywhere at once and had opinions on every subject. During one class, he interrupted the lecture so often that the weary professor finally shouted, "See here, Roosevelt, let me talk. I'm running this course."

He worked out with a boxing coach, wrestled, rowed a shell on the Charles River, and was chosen as a member of the exclusive Porcellian Club. He was on the editorial board of the *Harvard Advocate,* the student newspaper. He went to plays, concerts, and dances with a new circle of friends. He skated enthusiastically over the rough ice on the Charles River, exclaiming to a frozen companion, "Isn't this bully!" He tried to avoid the heavy drinkers on campus, taught Sunday school, and went bird watching with a friend.

While thoroughly enjoying life at Harvard, he remained tied to home. In a letter to his mother in the fall of 1876 he wrote, "Although I have enjoyed myself here . . . I do not think I have ever appreciated more the sweetness of home."

At the end of his freshman year, he went hiking in the Adirondack Mountains, then joined his family at Tranquility, the house his father had rented at Oyster Bay. There he spent the rest of the summer studying the birds of the area and publishing his findings in *Notes on Some of the Summer Birds of Oyster Bay.*

It was wonderful to be outside again. At Harvard his classes in natural science had not been what Ted had hoped for. He was used to being out in the woods observing nature. But at Harvard he was forced to sit through long lectures indoors and spend hours peering through microscopes in a laboratory. At the end of the summer, he discussed the matter with his father. Should he pursue a career as a naturalist? He would never make much money in the field, his father advised him, and

Theodore *(top right)* with other editors of the *Harvard Advocate*, the college newspaper. His activities also included crew, boxing, football, debating, bird watching, teaching Sunday School, and writing several chapters of a naval history. He was also elected to Phi Beta Kappa, a national academic honor society.

he must be prepared to give up some of the luxuries that he was used to. But if he loved the subject and was willing to dedicate himself to the highest quality of work, then he should go ahead. Ted returned to Harvard determined to become a natural scientist.

His letters home from college that autumn were filled with news about new friends, antics in the dining room, girls he met, exams, bird watching, sports, and books he was reading. But in the spring his letters became more somber. His father, Theodore Roosevelt Sr., was seriously ill. "We have always been very fortunate...in having a father whom we can love and respect more than any other man in the world," he wrote to Bamie. While Ted continued his classes in Cambridge, back in

New York the rest of the family watched helplessly as Theodore Sr. suffered from excruciating pain. It was clear he was dying, and Ted was called home. But he arrived too late to say good-bye to his father, who died on February 9, 1878, while Ted was en route.

Ted was grief stricken. His father had been "the best man I ever knew," he said. Ted's days felt like a "hideous dream." The joy he had discovered at Harvard was overshadowed now by the void left by his father's death. His diary was filled with concerns for his inability to live up to his father's standards.

His return to Tranquility in the summer of 1878, after his sophomore year, was bittersweet. He loved Oyster Bay, but everywhere he looked he was reminded of his father. But being outdoors always brightened Ted's outlook on life. Here he could tramp the woods, row across Long Island Sound (a twenty-five-mile roundtrip), and gallop through the woods on his horse, Lightfoot. To challenge himself even more, he spent the last few weeks of his summer vacation in the north Maine woods. His guide, Bill Sewall, took one look at Ted and guessed that the skinny young man with the thick glasses would never be up to the rigors of life in the wild. But after a thirty-mile hike in the rain and nights spent sleeping on the muddy ground, he was impressed. Ted Roosevelt was tougher than he looked.

During his junior year of college, his life took a new turn. Many people in his family assumed he would marry Edith Carow, Corinne's good friend and one of Ted's favorite childhood companions. But now he fell head over heels in love with Alice Lee, the lively blue-eyed daughter of a wealthy Boston banker. He needed his horse from home sent up to school, he wrote to Bamie. With Lightfoot stabled near-by, he could ride out to Chestnut Hill, where Alice lived in her family's mansion. He took Alice to lunch at the Porcellian Club, defying the males-only rule. They went to dances, rode a sleigh to the snow-covered countryside, and visited Ted's family in New York. She called him Teddy. And he wrote of her in his diary as "my sweet love."

It looked as though Teddy wanted to spend all his time with Alice—but he could never resist a camping trip. When March came, while there was still three feet of snow on the ground in Maine, Ted headed north to hunt. With Bill Sewall again as his guide he snowshoed, set traps, shot his first deer, and endured temperatures of −10 degrees Fahrenheit. "I have never passed a pleasanter two weeks," he reported enthusiastically in a letter to his mother.

At Harvard he gave up the idea of becoming a natural scientist. He would need a larger income if Alice agreed to marry him. Besides, he found he was more interested in his courses on politics than in natural science. And he was fascinated by history, especially naval history. He had found an error in a history book about Britain's naval war of 1812 and set out to write his own more accurate account of the event.

Another summer vacation at Tranquility and weeks away from Alice made Ted even more determined to win a commitment from her. He would be a senior in the fall of 1879, and he knew he wanted her as his wife. Alice, though, was causing him to lose sleep. He had proposed, but she was taking her time making up her mind. "See that girl?" he asked a friend. "I am going to marry her. She won't have me, but I am going to have *her!*" When Alice finally said yes in January, Roosevelt was ecstatic. "How she, so pure and sweet and beautiful can think of marrying me I can not understand, but I praise and thank God it is so," he wrote. With Alice at his side, life would always "seem laughing and loving."

Ted had a secret, though. The campus doctor told him in the spring of his senior year that he had a serious heart condition, caused by his childhood asthma. As a result, he should never engage in strenuous activity. Ted decided to keep the information to himself, not telling anyone until years later.

Pushing the doctor's warning aside, Ted plunged into a giddy round of parties, trips to New York, and graduation activities. In recognition of his academic achievements, he was elected to Phi Beta Kappa, an honor society, and graduated with honors in June 1880. Then on his twenty-second birthday, October 27, 1880, he and Alice were married in an elegant ceremony near Boston.

New York would be their home, the newlyweds decided, and they moved into a third-floor apartment in the Roosevelt family mansion on West Fifty-seventh Street. Theodore enrolled in Columbia Law School, which was then located downtown, near Washington Square. Each morning he strode briskly three miles south, then three miles back after his classes. The walk took him forty-five minutes each way.

He worked on his naval history manuscript, and he and Alice took a belated honeymoon, sailing for Europe in May 1881. Alice was seasick on the ship going over but rallied for sightseeing in Ireland, England, and Italy and for shopping in Paris. Teddy left her long enough to climb the Matterhorn, the highest mountain in the Swiss Alps. It was, he reported, "like going up and down enormous stairs on our hands and knees for nine hours."

Having conquered one of the world's most difficult peaks, he was ready for new challenges.

At twenty-three, Theodore Roosevelt ran for the state assembly from New York City's wealthy "Silk Stocking District." He won by a wide margin, becoming the youngest man ever elected to the assembly. He was in his element in Albany, fighting for government reforms, but he missed his wife, Alice.

16 ☆

Chapter 2

"DARLING WIFIE"

Theodore and Alice were one of New York's most popular young couples—sophisticated, witty, and rich. Almost every night their horse-drawn carriage clip-clopped through the streets of Manhattan, carrying them to an opera, a ball, a dinner, or a play. Theodore dressed for a night out in a cutaway jacket that fit smartly over his formal high-necked shirt. His shiny patent-leather shoes were ready to glide over the polished floors of New York's most fashionable ballrooms. Alice was dazzling in her beautiful gowns and jewels.

Theodore, though, often disappeared shortly before they were due at a social gathering. Dressed in his formal clothes, he would dash out of the house and head for a smoke-filled room above a saloon on East Fifty-ninth Street. There he climbed the worn wooden steps and entered a room filled with plumbers, streetcleaners, and saloonkeepers. His wealthy, aristocratic friends would never have associated with such men, but they were important to Roosevelt. They were the leaders of Morton Hall, the headquarters of the Twenty-first District Republican Association. They ruled the city and New York State. And Roosevelt wanted to be one of them.

Many of his friends were shocked. Good families, they told him, had nothing to do with politics. They told him that politics were "low" and the organizations were "not controlled by gentlemen." Roosevelt, though, was not about to be stopped.

The working-class men who gathered at Morton Hall were surprised to have Roosevelt join their ranks. But when he kept showing up at meetings, eager to become involved, they began to pay attention to him. The Republicans were used to being outvoted and outmaneuvered by the Democrats in the state legislature in Albany. Roosevelt was a new face. He was bright, energetic, honest, and rich. Why not ask him to run for state assemblyman?

Roosevelt accepted the offer, and in November 1881 he was elected assemblyman from the Twenty-first District of Manhattan. People called it the "Silk Stocking District" because of the fashionable high society that lived there. Theodore Roosevelt was the perfect man to represent them.

On the first day of the legislative session in Albany, Roosevelt entered the ornate new state capitol outfitted in formal clothes: a silk top hat, tails, and a gold-headed cane. He stepped confidently into the assembly hall, his hair parted in the middle, his sideburns carefully groomed, and a monocle on a gold chain glinting in one eye.

"Who's the dude?" one amused assemblyman asked dryly.

When Roosevelt introduced himself, his voice was high-pitched, almost screechy. Members of the legislature were to get used to that voice. Throughout his first term in office, Roosevelt often rose to his feet, leaned forward over his desk, and interrupted debates with a loud, insistent "Mistah Speekah."

In Albany, Roosevelt was in a different world from his circle of New York and Harvard friends. His fellow assemblymen were butchers, farmers, liquor-store owners, carpenters—even a former pickpocket. Roosevelt admired men who worked hard for a living. But most of these men were corrupt. They were, he wrote indignantly in his diary, "a stupid, sodden, vicious lot . . . deficient in brains and virtue."

The old-timers in the legislature underestimated the new young assemblyman from Manhattan. Roosevelt was a naive, arrogant showoff, they decided. But they couldn't ignore him. He introduced bills to make elections more honest. He wanted big business to get out of state and city affairs. Every chance he got, he talked with reporters about his ideas for reforming government. His name began appearing in newspapers almost every day.

Then he took on Jay Gould. Gould was one of the most powerful men in America. He had made a fortune in the railroad industry and had ties to Tammany Hall, a Democratic political club that persuaded immigrants and other low-paid workers to vote for its candidates. In exchange, the voters received jobs. Those who were elected then rewarded big business with lucrative state contracts. During President Ulysses S. Grant's term in office, Gould had rigged the gold market so that he got richer while the country plunged into a serious economic depression.

Roosevelt discovered that Gould had bought stock in the Manhattan Elevated Railroad at rock-bottom prices. Once the deal was complete, Gould had conspired with T. R. Westbrook, a state supreme court judge, to raise the company's stock price. Gould was then able to pocket millions of dollars.

Roosevelt heard of the scandal from a colleague, then spent hours poring through old newspaper reports to make sure the charges were true. Gould, after all, was one of the wealthy New York elite—like Roosevelt himself. But the rumors *were* true, Roosevelt decided. Gould had bought influence from a state supreme court judge in order to increase his own wealth at taxpayers' expense. Enraged, Roosevelt took to the floor of the assembly, lambasted Gould, and called for an investigation. The report that came back showed clearly that Gould and Westbrook had acted illegally. But members of the assembly, influenced by Gould's money, refused to impeach the judge.

The old-guard politicians were appalled at Roosevelt's brash attack, but the newspapers loved it. The colorful young assemblyman had livened up their beat and made great copy. Within weeks Roosevelt was known throughout the state as a young reformer leading the crusade for better government.

Roosevelt was in his element when he was fighting in Albany for what he believed in, but he missed Alice and life in New York City. During the week, he roomed in a seedy hotel occupied by other politicians. It was a far cry from the Roosevelt mansion on West Fifty-seventh Street or his room at Harvard. He didn't spend much time there, though. He became famous for his marathon hikes, and one man who walked with Roosevelt complained that he was so exhausted afterward he had to go to bed to recuperate.

Roosevelt also worked out regularly with a boxing coach. One night when he and some friends stopped by an Albany saloon, a Tammany Hall regular made some slighting remark about Roosevelt's clothes. In a flash Roosevelt hit the man and knocked him down. When the fellow got up, Roosevelt did it again—and then a third time. "When you are in the presence of a gentleman, conduct yourself like a gentleman," he angrily told the man.

Roosevelt's fighting spirit carried over to the floor of the legislature. When he returned to Albany after the annual election in January 1883 for his second term, the new governor called him into his office. Grover Cleveland was a Democrat, but like Roosevelt, he wanted to clean up New York State's government. Would Roosevelt help him do this? Within weeks Roosevelt had introduced several reform bills. He then worked with Cleveland to muster the votes to pass them.

Shuttling back and forth by train between Albany and New York, Roosevelt was busier than ever. Alice spent a few lonely weeks with him in Albany but then decided to stay in Manhattan. The two had a home of their own now, a brownstone on West Forty-fifth Street. Together on weekends, they rode out to Oyster Bay, where they spent hours hiking, boating, playing tennis, and visiting with relatives and friends. They loved Oyster Bay and bought land there so they could build a place of their own. They began plans for a twelve-bedroom house. Before it was finished, though, Roosevelt wanted to make a trip out west. "I am fond of politics," Roosevelt told a friend, "but fonder still of a little big-game hunting."

There were American buffalo, properly called bison, Roosevelt liked to point out, still roaming the Badlands of the Dakota Territory in 1883, and Theodore wanted to go see them for himself. He boarded a train headed west and arrived in the middle of the night in Little Missouri, a remote cattle town in what later became the state of North Dakota. He swung off the train and was directed to the Pyramid Park Hotel. There, sharing an overcrowded room with an assortment of snoring buffalo hunters, Roosevelt got his first taste of rough-and-tumble western life. The next day he found a hunting guide named Joe Ferris, and the two of them rode out into the Badlands in search of buffalo.

Roosevelt had heard about the millions of buffalo that crowded the western plains. Now, he and Ferris saw only carcasses and skeletons. Ranchers who drove herds of cattle north from Texas had claimed the grassland for their animals, starving buffalo to near extinction. Hunters shot buffalo for their valuable skins, and passengers on trains shot them just for sport, leaving the carcasses by the tracks.

At twenty-four, Theodore made his first trip to the Dakota Territory Badlands. He was a "regular cowboy dandy," he wrote to a friend, in his buckskin shirt and trousers and his alligator boots, with his engraved silver bowie knife from Tiffany's, New York City's finest jeweler.

The West that Roosevelt had read about and dreamed of was rapidly disappearing. The country needed a national conservation policy, he told a homesteader he met in Little Missouri. Still, he wanted a buffalo head of his own, and the next day he and Ferris headed out again on their hunt.

For two weeks the men endured thunderstorms, heavy rains, and fog. At night they slept on soggy, muddy ground. Their horses bolted and had to be chased down. The prairie winds howled day and night. Joe Ferris was miserable. But Theodore was having the time of his life. "After a week he was fresh as a daisy and I was dead beat," Ferris remembered later.

Finally, Theodore bagged his prize—a large buffalo bull. In triumph, he let out a war whoop and performed a victory dance while Ferris watched in amazement. Then Roosevelt skinned the animal and had the head shipped back home: It would make a good trophy mounted on a wall once the new home in Oyster Bay was completed.

Life in the rugged Dakota Territory had captured Roosevelt's imagination. Perhaps he could become a rancher, he mused, and hire Joe Ferris and his partner to oversee the operation while he was back east. The Northern Pacific had just built a rail line that serviced the area, so his cattle could easily be shipped to market. With money inherited from his father, Roosevelt purchased 450 head of cattle and the grazing rights to the Maltese Cross Ranch, then headed home.

In the fall of 1883 Theodore was reelected to serve a third term in the assembly. In New York he and Alice again went for carriage rides through Central Park, visited with friends, read to each other, and drove out to Oyster Bay, where they met with their architect and reviewed the plans for their new home. A book company published Theodore's *The Naval War of 1812*. Life seemed about perfect. Best of all, Alice was pregnant.

The assembly went into session, and Theodore, still promoting his reform causes, traveled to Albany during the week and returned to New York City on the weekends. When he was away in Albany, he wrote newsy, adoring letters home. "Darling Wifie," he wrote to Alice on February, 6, 1884. "How I did hate to leave my bright, sunny little love yesterday afternoon. I love you and long for you all the time."

A few days later he was back in Manhattan, but left again on Tuesday, February 12, 1884. He left early in the morning to board the northbound train for Albany. Alice, lonely in the new house on Forty-fifth Street, was now staying with Theodore's mother and sister on West Fifty-seventh Street, where she planned to deliver the baby. Wednesday morning, while he was at work on the floor of the assembly, Roosevelt received a telegram. Alice had delivered a healthy baby girl! He was ecstatic. He would introduce a few new bills, he said, before leaving to join

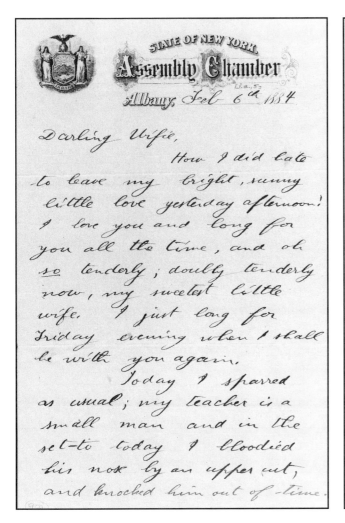

"Darling Wifie," TR wrote to Alice from the state assembly in Albany.

his wife and baby. The joy drained from his face, though, when a clerk handed him a second telegram. In a rush, he finished up his legislative work and boarded the next train to New York. Alice was not doing well, the second telegram had said. Come home at once.

Dense fog and rain covered the Northeast as Theodore made the excruciatingly slow trip from Albany to New York. When he reached the Roosevelt mansion on West Fifty-seventh Street, it was nearly midnight. Elliott met him at the door with more bad news. Alice was dying and, unbelievably, so was his mother.

Alice was barely conscious as Theodore held her in his arms until three in the morning. Then he left her bedside and walked downstairs to his mother's room. Mittie had seemed in good health earlier in the week, except for what appeared to be a serious cold. It was not a cold, though—it was typhoid fever, a deadly disease caused by contaminated food or water. In the late 1800s, it almost always meant certain death. Now, with all four of her children at her bedside, Mittie Roosevelt died. She was forty-six years old.

Numb with grief and confusion, Theodore returned to Alice's bedside, holding her failing body in his arms for several more hours. A serious kidney disease had gone undiagnosed throughout her pregnancy, and now it was too late to do anything to save her. At two in the afternoon Alice died. It was Valentine's Day 1884, and Theodore had lost the two most beloved women in his life.

Stunned by the tragedy, Theodore sat grimly through the double funeral, as the minister eulogized his mother and his twenty-three-year-old wife. Bamie, Theodore's sister, stepped in to take care of the baby, named Alice for her mother. Theodore seemed to have no interest in her. "For joy or sorrow, my life has now been lived out," he wrote in his diary.

His sisters worried that Theodore might actually go crazy with grief, but he was saved by his work. He was back in Albany two days after his wife's and mother's funeral. Those who tried to console him found they could not. A fellow assemblyman said, "You could not talk to him about it....He did not want anyone to sympathize with him."

Shuttling between New York City and Albany, Roosevelt conducted investigations of city corruption. He stayed up all night writing reports after his secretaries began to yawn and plead for sleep. He made impassioned speeches for government reform.

In April, just weeks after the death of his wife and mother, he traveled to Utica, where he gathered backing for Senator George Edmunds of Vermont. Edmunds was running for president as an independent Republican. Party regulars had divided their support between President Chester Arthur and James G. Blaine, a former secretary of state with a dubious reputation. They were not pleased with Roosevelt's opposition.

In the end, however, Roosevelt was so skillful in his political negotiations that he and three other independent Republicans were chosen to represent New York State at the national Republican convention in Chicago in June 1884. There, along with Henry Cabot Lodge, his friend and political ally from Boston, he campaigned vigorously for George Edmunds. For a while it seemed as if the independent Republicans would prevail. Finally, though, James Blaine took the lead among the delegates. When it looked as if Edmunds would lose, Roosevelt climbed on a chair and screamed at the other delegates until he was red in the face.

Disillusioned and exhausted, Roosevelt told reporters he was headed west. Reluctantly, he announced he would support Blaine, knowing it was his only chance of political salvation. His term in the assembly was finished, and he had no heart for running again. Besides, he had alienated the Republican Party regulars with his support of Edmunds. He feared that his political career was finished.

With the convention over, he headed for the Dakota Territory and his cattle. Perhaps there he could forget the tragic events of the past year.

Chapter 3

"THE WILD WEST"

Medora was a growing western cow town in 1884, located in the Dakota Territory. It had about one thousand residents, a rail line, and a meat-packing plant. Life in Medora was rough. Cattlemen feuded over stolen livestock; shootouts and fistfights at the local saloon were common. The summer sun scorched the already dry earth, and winter storms were ruthless. Ranch hands were uncouth and uneducated. Living conditions were harsh. It didn't seem like the place for a refined easterner. But Theodore Roosevelt took to it immediately.

His outfit probably caused some comment among the town's cowboys. Roosevelt loved clothes and spent a considerable amount of money on what he thought the well-dressed rancher should wear. He dressed, he wrote to a friend back east, in a broad sombrero, a fringed and beaded buckskin shirt, horsehide riding trousers, cowhide boots, and silver spurs. His revolver was gold- and silver-plated. His glasses made him look like a weakling. "Four eyes," some of the locals called him.

But Roosevelt was no East Coast tourist. He had come to Medora to work and to put down roots. His herd of cattle at the Maltese Cross Ranch had increased and now he bought the rights to new land, the Elkhorn Ranch, on the Little Missouri River north of Medora. Here in this idyllic spot he decided to build a ranch house for himself and his helpers. He persuaded his old hunting guide from Maine, Bill Sewall, and Bill's nephew Will Dow to come west to give him a hand. He hired two local ranchmen, Bill Merrifield and Sylvane Ferris, to help run his operation.

"It was still the Wild West in those days," he wrote years later in his auto-biography. "In that land we led a hardy life. Ours was the glory of work and the joy of living." During roundup time, he was in the saddle as long as eighteen hours a day helping with wrestling and branding calves. He was in the saddle before dawn, did not stop working until eight at night, and was up again before dawn the next morning.

In a letter to Henry Cabot Lodge, he described an outing on the Powder River. "My dear old Lodge," he wrote. "You must pardon the paper and general appearance of this letter, as I am writing out in camp, a hundred miles or so from any house; and indeed whether this letter is, or is not, ever delivered depends partly on Providence, and partly on the good will of an equally inscrutable personage, either a cowboy or a horse thief, whom we have just met, and who has volunteered to post it—my men are watching him with anything but friendly eyes, as they think he is going to try to steal our ponies."

Often Roosevelt worked a full day on the ranch, then went back to the cabin to read or write. There, in his rocking chair, he would read, write, or talk well into the night. According to his companions, he became so absorbed in what he was doing that he would often rock all around the cabin floor and back to his starting point.

Other times, Roosevelt hunted deer, grouse, elk, rabbit, and duck. In September 1884, he and Bill Merrifield spent weeks on foot, dressed in moccasins and buck-skins, tracking animals in the snow-capped Bighorn Mountains of Montana. His greatest triumph on the trip was killing a grizzly bear with one clean shot through its skull.

Slowly, he gained the respect of Medora's cowboys and ranchmen. He punched out a drunk in a bar for insulting his glasses. He was challenged to a duel by a nearby rancher but ended up becoming his friend.

Theodore was in better physical shape than he ever had been. His brown hair turned blond from the prairie sun, and his face became bronzed. He bought more cattle and spent hours working on the manuscript for a new book, *Hunting Trips of a Ranchman*.

He visited Long Island, spending time with Bamie and his young daughter. He inspected the house he and Alice had planned on building before her death. It was

After Alice's death, Roosevelt returned west. His cohorts were hard-living cowboys and ranchmen, shown here playing cards at the local hotel.

completed now. The couple had wanted to call it Leeholm, after Alice's family, but now he named it Sagamore Hill.

When he returned west, he lived on the Elkhorn Ranch, which he shared with Bill Sewall and Will Dow. The two men had brought their wives and Bill's three-year-old daughter from Maine, and they were, Roosevelt wrote to Bamie, "a very happy little family."

In the early spring of 1886 his fighting spirit was roused when two thieves stole a boat from his ranch. Immediately, he and Bill Sewall built a new boat and set out in pursuit. After several days they found the thieves, and Roosevelt spent six days and nights guarding the men as they made the uncomfortable journey down the ice-jammed river. Then, for forty-five tortuous miles, Roosevelt marched in freezing weather behind a wagon carrying the thieves into town, where he turned them over to the sheriff. The boat the men had stolen was not valuable, but Roosevelt could not stand the thought of anyone breaking the law. Never one to travel without a book, he read Leo Tolstoy's hefty *Anna Karenina* during the trip and later wrote a thorough critique of the novel in a letter to his sister Bamie.

All in all, Theodore was thoroughly enjoying his life as a rancher and a cowboy. He finished one book and started writing another, and became active in a local ranchman's association. He delivered a Fourth of July speech in a nearby town, declaring himself "at heart as much a westerner as an easterner."

But the cattle business had not flourished as he had hoped. Prices were down, and the plains were overgrazed. Sell the herd, Bill Sewall advised him in the fall of 1886. There was no profitable future in the Badlands. Sewall and Dow wanted to return to Maine and thought that Roosevelt would lose his investment if he did not get out of the cattle business.

Roosevelt did not sell the herd, though. In early October 1886 he left Medora and returned to New York City. Bill Sewall closed up the Elkhorn Ranch and headed back to Maine. The upcoming winter would bring disaster to the plains of the Badlands. Within five months of Roosevelt's departure, most of his herd, along with virtually all the cattle of the Dakota Territory, was gone.

The blizzard began in November 1886. When the snow came, it was so fierce it piled up in drifts of seven feet overnight. Temperatures dropped to more than −40 degrees Farenheit. The snow kept on falling through December and into January. Now the drifts were more than a hundred feet deep. Then, at the end of January 1887, a new blizzard descended, more bitter than any in history. Ranchers left their cabins, only to die within minutes. Some of those who stayed inside went mad or killed themselves.

Cattle died from lack of oxygen when their nostrils filled with snow and ice. Their hooves became trapped in the crusted snow, and unable to move, they froze to death. Those that survived made their way into the towns, bellowing in fear and anguish. People in Medora nailed boards across their windows to keep the animals from breaking through the glass in their desperate search for food and warmth. In

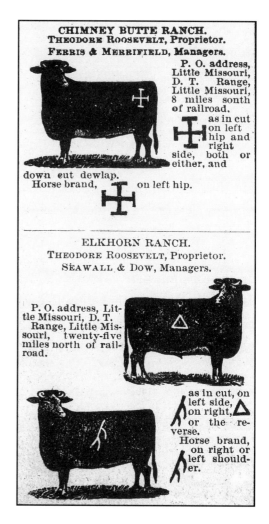

In the Badlands, Roosevelt worked alongside seasoned wranglers rounding up cattle for branding, once spending forty hours in the saddle. His Chimney Butte (also called Maltese Cross) and Elkhorn ranch brands are shown here.

March, when the spring thaw finally came, there was little left of the majestic herds that had held so much promise for their owners. Roosevelt lost almost all his cattle and much of the inheritance from his father that he had invested in his ranch.

The blizzard put an end to Roosevelt's life as a rancher. But Elkhorn, the Badlands, and the West were now an essential part of his character. He had pitted himself against the elements and grown stronger. He had made valued friends among seasoned cowboys, who bore no resemblance to his privileged friends back east. He had made some money—and had lost a lot. He had hunted big game, learned the songs of dozens of new birds, and heard the lonely cry of the wolves at night. He had seen the beauty of the unexplored wilderness and knew the nation must move swiftly to save its forests and streams from destruction.

And it was at the Elkhorn Ranch that Theodore was finally able to write about his lost Alice. On the banks of the Little Missouri, in the comforting company of the cottonwoods and the mourning doves, he composed a brief, eloquent memorial to her. She was, he wrote, "beautiful in face and form, and lovelier still in spirit. . . . Fair, pure, and joyous as a maiden; loving, tender, and happy as a young wife; when she had just become a mother, when her life seemed so bright before her—then, by a strange and terrible fate, death came to her."

He never wrote or spoke of her again—not to his daughter, his family, or his friends. When his daughter was grown, she said that it was her Aunt Bamie, not her father, who told her stories of her beautiful, charming mother. And Theodore, writing his own memoirs decades later, never even mentioned Alice Lee or his marriage to his "Darling Wifie."

Chapter 4

"MY LITERARY WORK"

In New York, Roosevelt turned from cattle to politics. Instead of saddling up and riding the range, he drove through the streets of the city in a horse-drawn carriage.

And he had a secret. He was engaged to be married again. No one was supposed to know, not even Bamie. He feared that people might think he was being disloyal to the memory of Alice. But when he had visited Bamie's New York townhouse in the fall of 1885, he had run into Edith Carow, his old childhood friend and playmate. He was captivated by her. She had been leaving just as he was entering. It must have been a little awkward. He had, after all, known her all his life, and many people had thought they were sweethearts. But he had chosen to marry Alice. He and Edith had been romantically involved years before, he confided to Bamie, but they had broken up because they both had "tempers that were far from being the best."

Now he was thoroughly in love again. He secretly began to court Edith, referring to her in his diary only by the initial "E." Before he returned west and she sailed for Europe, they planned for their marriage in London the following year.

Romance was back in his life. So, too, was politics. The seat for the mayoralty of New York was open, and much to Roosevelt's surprise, state Republican Party leaders asked if he would be willing to run. Now that his ranching days were over, he was ready to say yes. There was strong competition from the two opponents,

Henry George, the Labor Party candidate, and the Democrats' choice, Abram S. Hewitt. But if Roosevelt could attract some of the reform Republican voters away from the Labor candidate, the Republicans might have a chance of winning.

Roosevelt was a natural campaigner. He knew how to delay his entrance into a hall until the audience was eager for his appearance. He knew how to lean forward, raise his fist and his voice, and rail against his opponents. He knew how to appeal to special blocs of voters. He campaigned among African Americans and assured immigrant workers that he would strive to improve their lives.

In November, though, Abram Hewitt was elected the new mayor, and Roosevelt finished last. Under any other circumstances Roosevelt might have been devastated, but he was headed for a new adventure. Putting his defeat behind him, he stepped aboard an ocean liner and sailed for England. There, on December 2, 1886, in a private ceremony in a little church in London, he and Edith Carow were married. She had been a constant companion when he was growing up. Now she would be his companion for life.

With a new wife to support, Theodore Roosevelt needed a job. He had lost money in his western cattle venture and had just taken an expensive four-month honeymoon throughout Europe. Life in New York was more expensive than life on the ranch in the Dakota Territory. There was now a large household to run, guests to entertain, servants to be paid, formal clothes to be bought, and a nursemaid to be hired for young Alice.

And there was Sagamore Hill, the house at Oyster Bay. He loved the rambling structure, with its wraparound porch and views of Long Island Sound. But it had cost much more than he had anticipated.

Although Roosevelt came from a wealthy family, he was spending more than he took in. Edith would do her best to change that. She soon learned, however, that her exuberant husband had little sense about money. And right now, he needed income. He would write another book, he decided, a biography of Gouverneur Morris, one of the framers of the U.S. Constitution.

He had the perfect place for it. At Sagamore Hill he could work close to Edith, his daughter Alice, and the Long Island forests he had tramped as a boy. He had a good view of the water from the window where he wrote—but he moved his desk

On December 2, 1886, Roosevelt married Edith Carow, his childhood playmate.

away from it so that he would not be distracted. Once he began the book, he wrote steadily, sometimes all day, taking breaks only to play with Alice and her new half brother, Theodore Jr., born in September 1887.

After months of researching, writing, and rewriting, Theodore was ready for some outdoor life. In late 1887, he took a hunting trip in the Badlands, where he spent several weeks alone in the mountains. Without companions, he was able to savor the stillness of the forest and the rich blue skies above. But where was the big game he was used to finding on his earlier trips? The cattle were gone from the area, due in part to the previous year's blizzard. So, too, were the bear, the antelope, and the buffalo. Extreme weather, overgrazing, and hunters—Roosevelt among them—had thinned the herds of wildlife that had once been so plentiful. It was tragic, Roosevelt thought, that these noble animals, one of America's greatest heritages, were disappearing.

When he returned to New York, Roosevelt shared his concern with his friend, the editor of *Forest and Stream* magazine, George Grinnell. Together they founded the Boone and Crockett Club, dedicated to saving what was left of the country's big-game and natural forests. The group focused first on Yellowstone National Park. Congress had made the vast stretch of unspoiled wilderness a national park in 1872. But there were no laws to protect the park from developers and hunters. A railroad company planned to bring thousands of tourists to a big new hotel. Developers had built a sawmill in the park and cut hundreds of trees for lumber. Pollutants poured into the streams. Hunters slaughtered rare animals. Visitors and workers scrawled their names on the park's dramatic rock formations.

With Roosevelt at the helm, the Boone and Crockett Club pushed Congress to protect Yellowstone. The group also helped create zoos in New York City and Washington, D.C. It lobbied for the creation of bird and animal preserves and protection for endangered trees in the West. The club also supported passage of a new federal law, the Forest Reserve Act of 1891, which gave the president of the United States the authority to set aside certain wooded areas as federal lands, protecting them from development.

By 1888 Roosevelt considered himself a writer rather than a politician. "Like yourself, I shall probably never be in politics again," he wrote to a former colleague from the New York State Assembly. "My literary work occupies a good deal of my time."

He had begun thinking about an idea for a new book—a series of books, in fact. He would tell the history of the American West. Enthusiastically, he began poring through old letters, journals, and maps. He was a "literary fellow" now, he told his friends. But when, in the fall of 1888, the nation elected Benjamin Harrison, a Republican, as president, Roosevelt's interest in politics suddenly perked up again.

Might there be a job for him in the new administration, Roosevelt asked Henry Cabot Lodge, his long-time friend, who was now a senator from Massachusetts. Assistant secretary of state, perhaps? No, came the answer. The leaders in the Republican Party had long memories: Roosevelt had not backed the party's favorite in the 1884 election. They were not about to reward him with an important job now.

There was a job with the Civil Service Commission, however. But Lodge didn't think Roosevelt would be interested: the pay was very low and the commission was almost unheard of—a sleepy, do-nothing organization. Roosevelt surprised Lodge. He said yes.

Chapter 5

"WE STIRRED THINGS UP"

Roosevelt bounded up the steps two at a time as he headed toward his new office in Washington. He was a man in a hurry, a man with a mission. Who knew how long he might be in the nation's capital? Politicians here came and went, lasting only as long as the work they did pleased the president who had appointed them. Roosevelt planned to shake up the sleepy Civil Service Commission and bring it to the country's attention. And he planned to do it fast.

The Civil Service Commission was in charge of filling government jobs. Both Republicans and Democrats used the system to reward loyal party workers. If a saloonkeeper organized the patrons at his bar to show up at the polls and vote for a certain candidate, he might soon have a high-paying job in that city's post office. If a businessman gave money to a presidential candidate, he might be appointed to a powerful position in Washington. It didn't really matter whether these people had the necessary skills for their jobs. This practice of appointing loyal supporters to public offices was called "the spoils system," and Roosevelt hated it. So did thousands of other Americans.

Reform! The civil service system needed reforming, and Roosevelt thought he was the man to do it. There were two other commissioners, but Roosevelt immediately plunged in to take the lead. He knew a thing or two about state and city reform from his days as a New York assemblyman. Now he wanted to reform the federal system as well.

Eagerly, Roosevelt began exposing abuses in the civil service system. In New York, applicants for jobs at the customs house could buy the answers to the civil service exam for fifty dollars if they knew the right person. In Indianapolis, the postmaster general had fired Democrats and replaced them with loyal Republicans—even though one of them was the boss of an illegal gambling ring.

Roosevelt visited Indiana and called for an investigation. "We stirred things up well," he wrote to Henry Cabot Lodge from Washington in June 1889. "The President has made a great mistake in appointing a well-meaning, weak old fellow …but I think we have administered a galvanic shock that will reinforce his virtue for the future." President Harrison, who was from Indianapolis and was a good friend of the postmaster general, must have wondered why he had ever appointed Roosevelt to this job.

But Roosevelt didn't stop. Next he took on the postmaster general of Wisconsin, who had changed the results of civil service exams in order to appoint his own favorites. Roosevelt set to work to have him ousted. He hadn't counted on John Wanamaker, however.

Wanamaker was a wealthy Philadelphia businessman who had poured thousands of dollars into Harrison's campaign and had been rewarded with the job of postmaster general of the entire country. Wanamaker thought the spoils system kept the Republican Party strong and had replaced thousands of Democrats in the postal system with party loyalists. According to him, Roosevelt was nothing but a self-righteous showman. Many members of Congress, both Republicans and Democrats, shared this opinion.

Congress called for an investigation into Roosevelt's tactics. Hadn't he told a witness in the Wisconsin case that he would protect his job if the man testified against his boss? Of course he had, Roosevelt thundered. If the system was ever to be cleaned up, witnesses needed to be protected and assured that they would not lose their income. Congress decided that Roosevelt had done no wrong, and the newspapers hailed him as a hero. Wanamaker, however, continued to view Roosevelt as an enemy of the Republican Party.

Roosevelt loved his new life in Washington. He could hobnob with the men who ran the country—diplomats, senators, cabinet members, historians, and writers.

Dressed in formal evening clothes, he dined at the lavish mansions that lined the capital's tree-shaded streets and made friends with some of the most influential men in the country. On weekends, he rode out to Rock Creek Park for vigorous hikes. He scrambled through the rugged terrain and plunged across streams to scale fifty-foot-high rock cliffs. Anyone courageous enough to go along with him came home exhausted. In addition, two volumes of his history, *The Winning of the West,* had been published and praised.

Life in Washington was expensive, though, and Roosevelt was straining to make ends meet. He had a second son now, Kermit, born in October 1889. To save money during his first two years in Washington, he lived with the Lodges, shuttling between the capital and Oyster Bay to be with his family. Finally, he found a small but fashionable house he could afford to rent, and Edith and the children joined him.

He was in his early thirties now, a rising young reformer with an attractive wife and children. But he was in trouble with his party and with President Harrison. And the Harrison administration itself was in trouble. It looked as if the president might be defeated in the upcoming election.

In Baltimore, the city's postmaster ordered his employees to contribute part of their salaries to Harrison's campaign. If they didn't, they would lose their jobs. Roosevelt headed for Baltimore on the day of the primary elections. Everywhere he turned he saw corruption: Poll watchers and voters were openly bribed so they would vote for Harrison, and government workers hauled unregistered voters to the polls. The people involved were more than willing to talk. Sure, they engaged in illegal campaign practices, they told Roosevelt. Wasn't that the way it was done?

Roosevelt wrote a scathing report of the government corruption in Baltimore and recommended that twenty-five political appointees be fired. No one in the administration, especially his enemy John Wanamaker, wanted to see the report. Roosevelt had done enough harm to the party already. Get rid of him, congressmen advised Harrison. But the president had other matters on his mind. His wife was dying, and he was losing his bid for reelection. When Roosevelt's report finally became public, Wanamaker and the political appointees in Baltimore were disgraced. Roosevelt had triumphed again.

The Republicans no longer had to worry about getting rid of Roosevelt when Grover Cleveland, a Democrat, was elected president in 1892. Surely, he would not want to keep such a troublemaker in office. But Cleveland surprised everyone, including Roosevelt. He knew Roosevelt from their days in New York State government and wanted the young reformer to stay on. So for two more years Roosevelt headed up the commission. But when he was offered a job as police commissioner in New York City, he leaped at the chance.

Chapter 6

"MAN'S WORK"

New York City's police department was famous in 1895 for its corruption. Gamblers, thieves, prostitutes, and murderers briskly pursued their trade while members of the police force looked the other way. Saloonkeepers sold liquor on Sunday, even though it was against the law. They had, after all, paid off the officers on the beat who were supposed to close them down.

Police Chief Thomas Byrnes had become rich from taking bribes. Policemen throughout the ranks followed his example, and more than street criminals were involved in the payoffs. Business owners and shopkeepers made regular "contributions" to police officers for protection against crime. Wealthy Wall Street bankers rewarded Chief Byrnes with insider tips on the stock market in exchange for keeping thieves from robbing their banks. Byrnes did this through his connections with the city's criminals. The police would look the other way, he told them, as long as they committed crimes in other parts of the city and left the banks alone. And they must stay away from the "frozen zone," a square mile that encompassed the Wall Street financial district. If they were seen there, they would be arrested immediately. It was how the "system" worked, and it had been in place for years.

The system "will break you," Chief Byrnes told Roosevelt when the new commissioner arrived at the busy police headquarters at 300 Mulberry Street. "You will yield. You are but human." But Byrnes underestimated Roosevelt, who was elected president of the commission shortly after his arrival.

Within weeks Chief Byrnes was gone, fired by Roosevelt and the other members of the commission, who looked on with awe—and sometimes anger—as Roosevelt charged ahead with his reforms. "I have the most important, and the most corrupt, department in New York on my hands.…Yet in spite of the nervous strain and worry, I am glad I undertook it; for it is man's work," he wrote to his sister Bamie in May 1895.

Roosevelt thrived on the constant buzz of activity at police headquarters. Located in the midst of the bustling Little Italy section of the city, the building was a gathering spot for newspaper reporters, police officers, detectives, secretaries, and

Roosevelt was hailed as a reformer, as shown in this cartoon, when he joined the New York City Police Commission.

political hangers-on. Politics played a big role in running the police department. Honesty and job qualifications did not.

Roosevelt set out to shake things up. He began by hiring a woman as his secretary, an unheard-of move at the time. He brought new policemen into the force based on the results of qualifying exams rather than on their political connections. When he learned that an immigrant had rescued women and children from a burning building, he encouraged him to take the exam. He was just the kind of man the police force needed, Roosevelt told him.

When an anti-Semitic German came to New York to deliver an address attacking Jews, he demanded special police protection. The speaker planned to "preach a crusade against the Jews," Roosevelt wrote later in his autobiography, and Jews in the city wanted Roosevelt to prevent him from speaking and deny him police protection. Not possible, Roosevelt told them. Besides, it would only make the speaker a martyr. "The proper thing to do," Roosevelt wrote, "was to make him ridiculous," so he assigned a Jewish sergeant and dozens of Jewish patrolmen to the event. "He made his harangue against the Jews under the active protection of some forty policemen, every one of them a Jew!"

Roosevelt was determined to clean up the police department and find new ways to fight crime more efficiently. He put a stop to the corrupt practice of policemen being able to buy their promotions. He hired minorities and required pistol practice and physical exams. He directed the detectives on the force to use the new Bertillion system, a method used in France of identifying criminals by their bone structure. He had a telephone system installed at headquarters and established a bike patrol.

The city began to sit up and take notice of the new man in charge. Stories about Roosevelt's surprise midnight prowls through the streets of Manhattan became legends. After an elegant dinner at the Union Club, Roosevelt would wrap himself in a dark cape, pull his hat down over his eyes, and join his friend, the journalist Jacob Riis, for some sleuthing on the back streets of the city. Their mission was to find and discipline policemen who were shirking their duties.

One summer night he and Riis heard a shopkeeper come out of his store in search of a policeman. "Where does that copper sleep?" the man muttered. On

An energetic administrator, Roosevelt shook up the New York police department by hiring female employees, introducing new technology for identifying criminals, and installing the headquarters' first phone system. At night he prowled the city's crime-ridden streets looking for corrupt or idle officers.

another excursion the two walked into a bar on the Upper East Side. "Why aren't you on your post, officer?" Roosevelt demanded of a policeman he found relaxing there. Wasn't he supposed to be on duty? The policeman ignored him. Roosevelt identified himself as the police commissioner, but the officer was unconvinced. The bartender, anxious to save his buddy from embarrassment, intervened. "It's his nibs himself," he declared to the patrolman. In seconds the policeman was out the door and back to work.

Soon policemen on the beat were on the lookout for Commissioner Roosevelt. It was his teeth that gave him away. They had become his trademark. Street vendors began selling model sets of teeth made to look like Roosevelt's. Political cartoonists drew the commissioner flashing a wide mouthful of choppers.

Roosevelt took reporters and journalists with him wherever he went on the job. And they helped educate him. Jacob Riis described to Roosevelt the horrible living conditions of New York City's immigrants and took him to visit the tenements on the Lower East Side. Reporters spent so much time in the commissioner's office that some people thought they were members of his staff. They had been with him when he bounded up the stairs to his office on his first day and demanded, "What do we do now?" The articles they wrote about him were full of praise. Working with Roosevelt was fun.

But not everyone loved Roosevelt. Some members of the press saw the old system crumbling, and they blamed Roosevelt for any crime that went unsolved. And when he took on the saloons of New York, his popularity plummeted.

According to New York law, bars were supposed to be closed on Sundays. But no one, neither saloonkeepers nor customers, paid any attention to the law. As long as bar owners paid bribes to the police officer patrolling their area, liquor could continue to flow freely, even on Sunday. Not anymore, Roosevelt announced. Selling alcohol on Sunday was a violation of the law, and as long as the law was on the books, he was going to enforce it.

The whole city was up in arms. Policemen weren't happy about enforcing a law they had previously ignored. Besides, they no longer could collect their bribes. Saloonkeepers were enraged at losing their Sunday trade. Tammany Hall political bosses, who profited from a lucrative relationship with the saloon owners, began a campaign against Roosevelt. And customers, who were used to spending the day in bars and relaxing with a drink or two, resented having their Sunday social life taken away from them. Roosevelt even received a letter bomb from an angry protester.

Roosevelt continued to support the enforcement of the law, unpopular though it was. But the leaders of the state's Republican Party weren't happy with the commissioner. Neither were the voters. And when state elections rolled around in November 1895, most of the offices in New York City went to Tammany Hall Democrats rather than Republicans.

Maybe, Roosevelt began to think, it was time to look for another job. He knew he was losing support as head of the police commission. When the Republican Party met in June 1896 to nominate William McKinley as its candidate for president, Roosevelt's interest turned toward national politics. It looked as if McKinley might win.

Reporter and photographer Jacob Riis took Roosevelt into the slums of New York's Lower East Side, giving him a firsthand glimpse of how thousands of immigrant workers lived.

For more than a year, Roosevelt continued his work in New York City. But when McKinley was elected president, Roosevelt began a campaign of his own. He wanted a job with the new administration. He had done what he had set out to do with the police force. Under his watch, crime in the city had decreased. He had increased the number of qualified police officers, and there was less corruption in the force. New standards were in place now, and the police headquarters operated more efficiently. And he had gained national attention with his reforms.

By April 1897, he was ready to take on a new challenge—one that would have a lasting impact on the nation and the world. He was ready to take on the U.S. Navy.

Chapter 7

"IMMENSE FUN"

The reception at the exclusive club in Washington was an elegant one: Women in fashionable gowns, men in high-collared white dress shirts and tails, and a guest list made up of the city's most elite society. Theodore Roosevelt, now assistant secretary of the navy, was in his element.

Talking a mile a minute in his screechy, high-pitched voice, he pounded his fist into his palm and waved his arms wildly as he expounded his views on U.S. military strategy. With one giant sweep of his hand he caught the dress of a nearby woman and accidentally ripped a decorative flower from her gown. The woman, a visitor from France, backed away in alarm, muttering *"Mon Dieu,"* My God. Roosevelt quickly delivered an abject apology in French to the startled woman and then turned to continue his rant against what he considered the weak-willed foreign policy of President McKinley.

Theodore Roosevelt wanted to go to war.

He had been appointed assistant secretary of the navy in April 1897, and after just a few months in office he had already made his mark in Washington. He had upstaged his boss, Secretary of the Navy John Long, and he was making President McKinley nervous with his outspoken views on foreign affairs.

Edith and the children were in Oyster Bay. There were two more young Roosevelts now, Ethel and Archie. Without his family with him in the capital, Roosevelt dined frequently at Washington's Metropolitan Club. There, surrounded by some of the capital's most influential politicians and military officers, he urged his friends to help make the United States a world power.

Roosevelt would order his favorite item on the menu—the double lamb chops—then lean forward earnestly to discuss the issues of the day. Spain still ruled Cuba and the Philippine Islands, he said. European powers had no right to be in the Western Hemisphere. And Japan—the United States must keep an eye on that country, the new assistant secretary of the navy warned his fellow diners. Japan had an impressive fleet of battleships compared with the United States. They had just conquered part of China and might move eastward into the Pacific. The United States should annex Hawaii before the Japanese did. The country needed to build a stronger navy and flex its muscle.

Everyone at the table agreed with Roosevelt's views. They were all expansionists and believed the United States should become a world leader. The country had become too comfortable, too materialistic. Americans were motivated by wealth and greed rather than by pride in their country, Roosevelt and his friends said. The country had forgotten how to fight for more noble goals.

One of the group, Colonel Leonard Wood, especially caught Roosevelt's attention. He had been an Indian fighter, had been with the expedition that captured the Apache chieftain Geronimo, and had received the Medal of Honor. In addition to being an excellent soldier, he was also a medical doctor. Like Roosevelt, he loved the West and he loved adventure. And he was a walker. Roosevelt was impressed by Wood's endurance. "He walked me off my legs," Roosevelt said admiringly.

Armed with bold ideas and the support of other expansionists, Roosevelt began shaking things up at the navy. His boss, Secretary Long, was a mild-mannered man and was glad to have Roosevelt take over the detailed operations of running the department.

Roosevelt wanted to know everything about his new assignment. He stood on the deck of the battleship *Iowa* as it steamed out of port on maneuvers and withstood the deafening blast of the ship's big guns. He pored over the complex details of the navy's various departments—maintenance, operations, personnel, supply, ordnance, contracting, and medical. He made friends with navy officers and staff.

To many it seemed that Roosevelt, not Long, was in charge of the U.S. Navy.

And Long, with his vigorous assistant at the helm, felt free to leave Washington and tend his garden in Massachusetts. The secretary would take off for weeks at a time, leaving Roosevelt in charge.

With Long out of the office, Roosevelt whirled into action. "The Secretary is away, and I am having immense fun running the navy," he wrote to a friend from Washington in August 1897.

The navy must be updated, he told anyone who would listen. He lobbied members of Congress, the White House, and the press. Japan, Britain, France, Spain, and Russia all had much stronger navies than the United States. If America ever wanted to become a world power, it must build new battleships, more cruisers, and

As assistant secretary of the navy, Theodore Roosevelt was a man with a mission: To make the United States a world power. Here he walks briskly past the White House on his way to his office.

more dry-dock facilities. He wrote memos, initiated investigations, and overhauled the procedures for hiring and training personnel. The navy, he believed, was key to making the United States the dominant power in the Western Hemisphere.

Back in 1823 President James Monroe had set out the Monroe Doctrine: The United States would not allow European powers to interfere in the affairs of the Western Hemisphere. In return, the United States would not get involved in Europe's colonies on the other side of the Atlantic. No one believed in the Monroe Doctrine more ardently than Roosevelt.

He made friends with the most influential newspaper editors in the country, enlisting them in his expansionist campaign. He spoke at military gatherings and at Groton, an exclusive private school in Massachusetts, where his young fifth cousin, Franklin, was a student. He regaled the class with hilarious tales of his days as New York City police commissioner and no doubt inspired them with his vision for a more dominant U.S. Navy. It was a "splendid" talk, Franklin reported in a letter to his mother. Inspired, Franklin began to chart his own life based on Cousin Theodore's.

Theodore's niece, Eleanor, was also influenced by her older relative. Shy and lonely, Eleanor was often intimidated by her rowdy cousins at Oyster Bay. And when Uncle Teddy enveloped her in one of his exuberant bear hugs, she hung back, embarrassed and uncomfortable. Aunt Edith, though, saw beyond young Eleanor's awkward shyness. "She may turn out to be a swan," she wrote to Bamie.

Theodore and Edith had five children now and a sixth on the way. America needed large families, Roosevelt believed. It was a patriotic duty to have lots of children. They would help build America. By the time Quentin, the youngest, was born, Theodore had rented a house in Washington for his expanding brood. His job at the Department of the Navy kept him on the go from early morning till late at night, and he wanted the family to be nearby.

Things were heating up in Cuba, and Roosevelt wanted the United States to intervene. Rebels there had risen up against Spain's oppressive rule, and Spain had responded with more cruelty. Peasants suspected of siding with the rebels were placed in concentration camps. Women and children starved or died from diseases, and Spanish soldiers burned the countryside. Americans sympathized with the Cuban rebels.

Cousins were always welcome at Sagamore Hill. Here sixteen young Roosevelts line up according to height. "Books are all very well in their way...but children are better than books," TR wrote in his autobiography.

U.S. newspapers were eager for a war that would boost their sales, and Cuba was the most likely place for war to erupt. Joseph Pulitzer and William Randolph Hearst owned two of New York City's most sensational newspapers, *The World* and the *New York Journal*. The two papers competed to print the most lurid headlines. Some of what they printed was true. Much of it, though, was inaccurate or exaggerated. But readers didn't care. They wanted Spain out of the Western Hemisphere and were ready for the country to go to war. So was Roosevelt.

Spain's ambassador to the United States, Enrique Depuy de Lome, was charming and friendly to his American hosts. But what he wrote back to Spain was quite another thing. McKinley is "weak and a bidder for the admiration of the crowd," he said in a letter to a friend on the other side of the Atlantic.

The letter was meant to be a private one, but instead it was intercepted and ended up on the front page of the *New York Journal*. What an outrage, people cried. Insulted, the American public called for an attack on Spanish forces in Cuba.

But President McKinley had been to war, the Civil War, the bloodiest war on record. He had no taste for leading the country into another battle. But he would not have the final word.

While the president dithered and Roosevelt fumed, the U.S. battleship *Maine* steamed from Key West, Florida, to Cuba. Riots had broken out in Havana, and American citizens there needed to be protected. McKinley hoped that Spain would take the arrival of the Maine as a friendly warning that the United States wanted a free Cuba and an end to the atrocities there.

On the evening of February 15, 1898, the *Maine* floated in Havana Harbor. The captain sat in his quarters, writing a letter to his wife. He heard the strains of the ship's bugler, the notes echoing across the water. It was 9:40 P.M. Everything seemed peaceful. Then, as he finished his letter, a thunderous explosion shook the vessel, shattering the hull. In an instant, more than 250 American sailors and officers were dead. Others were seriously wounded.

When the U.S. battleship *Maine* exploded in Cuba, Roosevelt overstepped his authority at the navy department and ordered the commanders of the U.S. ships to fuel up and prepare for battle.

The cause of the explosion was unknown. The ship's hold was full of ammunition. A simple spark could have set off the blast. There should be an investigation, the captain of the *Maine* cautioned. But Roosevelt, William Randolph Hearst, Joseph Pulitzer, and most Americans had already made up their minds: Spain was responsible for the disaster. "FOUL PLAY" sank the *Maine*, screamed the *World*'s headlines. "The *Maine* was sunk by an act of dirty treachery on the part of the Spanish," Roosevelt told a friend. "Remember the *Maine!* To hell with Spain!" became a rallying cry throughout the country.

President McKinley called for calm and ordered Congress to investigate the explosion. Roosevelt, though, took action. He waited until Secretary Long left the office one afternoon for a visit to his foot doctor. That left Theodore Roosevelt in charge of the U.S. Navy.

Commodore George Dewey was in command of the naval fleet in the Pacific. He and his fleet were currently stationed in Hong Kong. He must keep an eye on Spanish ships stationed near there, Roosevelt decided. "Keep full of coal," he cabled Dewey. In the event of a declaration of war with Spain, the fleet's duty would be to see that the Spanish squadron did not leave the Asiatic coast. He must keep the Spanish ships away from Cuba and also be prepared to do battle in the Philippine Islands, where the Spanish had troops. Then Roosevelt cabled other ships in the area, ordering them to stock up on coal, the fuel needed to power the ships, and deliver it to Dewey's fleet.

Roosevelt was not the one authorized to make these decisions. It was Long's duty. But the orders had been made, and they stood.

The investigators of the sinking of the *Maine* could not clearly identify the cause of the ship's explosion. Meanwhile, Roosevelt continued to charge ahead with preparations at the navy department. He purchased war vessels from other countries to fill in the gaps in the U.S. Navy and made it known that if the country went to war, "I want to go."

While McKinley continued to hesitate, Roosevelt disgustedly declared that the president had "no more backbone than a chocolate eclair." In the end, though, McKinley could not withstand the pressure to go to war. On April 25, 1898, Congress declared war on Spain.

Within days Roosevelt resigned his post as assistant secretary of the navy and began assembling a volunteer cavalry unit to fight the Spanish. Since he had no war experience himself, he asked his friend Leonard Wood to serve as colonel: Roosevelt would serve under him as lieutenant colonel. It seemed everyone wanted to join Roosevelt's regiment, and applicants poured in from all over the country. Exhilarated, Roosevelt found a training ground in San Antonio, Texas, ordered supplies, and began selecting recruits. He was finally living his childhood dream. Lieutenant Colonel Roosevelt was about to go to war.

Chapter 8

"A GREAT HISTORICAL EXPEDITION"

The Roosevelt children stood on the lawn at Oyster Bay watching their father. He was lying on his stomach, a rifle propped up in front of him as he fired away at a cardboard cutout of a Spanish soldier.

"Good shot," Archie called out, but his father shushed him. "Bunnies mustn't talk," he admonished the children sternly. Father needed to practice. Father was going to fight in the Spanish-American War and needed to perfect his target shooting, he told them.

Thousands of miles away in San Antonio, Texas, Colonel Leonard Wood mounted his horse and rode past a line of new recruits. They were a diverse crew—sophisticated college graduates, rugged cowboys, hardscrabble miners, artists, judges, and postal clerks. They had two things in common: They wanted to fight in Cuba in the war against Spain. And they were eager to follow Theodore Roosevelt into battle.

There were Ivy League chums of Roosevelt's: a quarterback from Harvard, a champion tennis player, a high jumper from Yale, the former captain of the Columbia crew. There were policemen who had served with Roosevelt in New York City. There were friends from his days on the Medora ranch. There were sheriffs, small-town mayors, and deputy marshals. There were old Indian fighters, and there were Indians.

It seemed everyone wanted to sign up for the Rough Riders, the nickname given

Roosevelt recruited the First U.S. Volunteer Cavalry Regiment to fight in the Spanish-American War in Cuba. Known as the Rough Riders, the men trained in San Antonio, Texas.

to the First U.S. Volunteer Cavalry Regiment headed by Colonel Wood and Lieutenant Colonel Roosevelt. They were a "splendid set of men," Roosevelt wrote later, "accustomed to handling wild and savage horses." Many of them had herded cattle or hunted big game, and they were "hardened to life in the open." Now it was Roosevelt and Wood's duty to train and equip them for the war against Spain.

Roosevelt arrived in dusty San Antonio in May 1898 wearing the new uniform he had ordered from Brooks Brothers. Some of the men were disappointed when they first saw him. He was wearing glasses—a sign of weakness, they feared. But soon the men in their wide-brimmed hats and neckerchiefs realized that Roosevelt was willing to do everything he asked of them. Along with the recruits, he rolled out of bed at 5:30 A.M. at the sound of the bugle. He shared a breakfast cooked over a campfire, then mounted his horse to lead the men in drills under the relentless Texas sun. At lunch he shared rations, and while the men broke in new horses, he and Wood requisitioned supplies from Washington. In the evenings, after the men had retired to their tents to sleep, Roosevelt was still awake, writing letters well into the night.

Roosevelt loved his men and was proud of them. But when he went with one of the squadrons to a local bar and bought a round of drinks for the entire crew, Colonel Wood was indignant. An officer who went out drinking with his men was "unfit to hold a commission," Wood said pointedly. Embarrassed, Roosevelt lamented, "I consider myself the damnedest ass within ten miles of this camp."

Soon, though, the troops had more serious matters to deal with. Orders arrived for the Rough Riders to herd their horses onto a train and make the steamy, four-day trip to the port city of Tampa, Florida. From there they would be shipped out, probably to Cuba and to battle.

Disappointment and chaos greeted the troops in Tampa. The Rough Riders had trained as a cavalry unit—they were horsemen. But, they learned when they arrived, only officers could take horses when they shipped out. Worse yet, not all of the men could go. There was room for only part of the regiment. The others would be left behind, unable to follow Roosevelt and Wood to Cuba.

And then there was the problem of finding a train that would take the men and horses from their tent encampment to the Tampa pier. When no train showed up, Roosevelt saw a string of grime-covered coal cars. They weren't there for the Rough Riders, and they were headed away from the pier. Never mind, Roosevelt decided. It was transportation. At his command, the men clambered on board and the train chugged nine miles in reverse to Tampa's port.

No one seemed to be in charge at the dock. Thousands of troops milled about, waiting for orders. Roosevelt, appalled by the lack of organization, learned that one ship, the *Yucatan*, had been assigned to two other regiments. But those troops

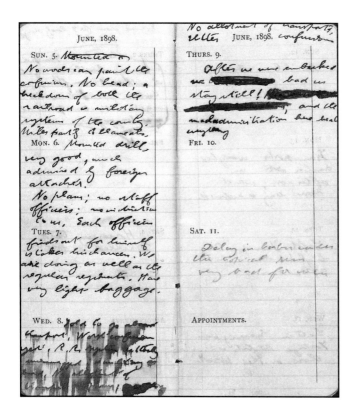

In Tampa, Florida, Roosevelt scribbled a water-stained entry in his journal describing the disorganized state of affairs as his troops prepared to sail for Cuba.

hadn't boarded yet. Roosevelt was not about to be left behind on the pier because of the military's incompetence, so he hurried the Rough Riders onto a launch that ferried them out to the *Yucatan*. It was theirs, the assigned regiments screamed from the pier. "Well," Roosevelt called back, standing safely on deck, "we seem to have it."

It was not an easy voyage. At first, it was not even a voyage. The American ships were warned to stay in Tampa Bay: Spanish ships were rumored to be in the Gulf of Mexico. For more than two weeks, troops on the *Yucatan*, sandwiched into cramped, unsanitary quarters, sweltered on board while Roosevelt angrily paced the deck. Finally, the ships steamed out of Tampa Bay and headed toward Cuba's Santiago Harbor. Despite the hardships, Roosevelt was in high spirits. "It is a great historical expedition," he wrote to his sister Corinne from the Gulf of Mexico on June 15, 1898, "and I thrill to feel I am a part of it."

The first challenge for the Rough Riders in Cuba was unloading men, supplies,

On board the *Yucatan*, the Rough Riders waited for days in excruciating heat and overcrowded conditions before they were permitted to sail to Cuba. "Standing room only," one soldier wrote on the side of the ship. Another scrawled, "And damned little of that."

and horses from the *Yucatan* at Daiquiri, a small village east of Santiago. There was only a rickety wooden pier, which made disembarking difficult. Some men chose to swim ashore. As waves smashed against the ship's hull, soldiers struggled to board the small landing craft that bobbed crazily in the heavy surf. Two men drowned. Most of the horses, frightened and confused, thrashed their way to shore. Roosevelt, who had brought two horses with him on the ship, saw one of them drown as the surf washed over the animal's head.

Once on shore the sodden troops gathered their supplies and set up camp for the night on the beach. Some supplies, including food, water, blankets, and ammunition, were lost during the landing. Roosevelt had managed to save his toothbrush and the nine extra pairs of eyeglasses he had sewn into his clothes.

The next morning the march to a nearby fishing village began. The Rough Riders had trained as horsemen, not foot soldiers, and the seven-mile trek through the Cuban jungle was torture. The heat and humidity sapped their energy as they labored up the steep hills. Rough coral rocks tore into their feet. They had expected to ride into battle. Instead, they tramped.

Roosevelt could have ridden. He was an officer and had his horse with him. But he believed that good officers never asked their men to do things they themselves would not do. So for seven tortuous miles the Rough Riders snaked their way through the hills with Roosevelt, sweating profusely inside his yellow slicker, leading the way.

When the men finally reached the village, they were ordered to turn north and head toward Las Guasimas, a mountain pass where more than two thousand Spanish soldiers were encamped. The vegetation was dense. Occasional notes from a bugle drifted through the jungle, signaling that other U.S. troops were nearby. There were strange bird calls that even Roosevelt, an expert in bird lore, did not recognize.

Suddenly, as the men paused for a few moments' rest, the air was thick with bullets. Guerrillas hiding in the jungle had spotted the Rough Riders. Using the eerie bird calls the men had heard, they had communicated the Rough Riders' location up to the Spanish troops who lay in wait at the top of the mountain pass.

For two and a half hours the Spanish rained gunfire down on American troops as the Rough Riders and other regiments struggled up the hillside toward them. Two of Roosevelt's favorite junior officers were whirled around by the impact of oncoming bullets, then fell dead. Others lay wounded and writhing in pain. Bark flew from a tree and momentarily blinded Roosevelt as his men made for a clearing. Although the Americans were outnumbered almost two to one, the Rough Riders fired with deadly accuracy, and finally the Spanish soldiers fled west toward Santiago.

Now the word came down from General William Shafter, the officer in charge of U.S. land troops. The men were to fall back and reconnoiter. So for days the men sweltered in the jungle, fighting off land crabs and insects. Many of them had thrown away their heavy blankets and bedrolls as they trudged through the jungle. Now they slept on bare ground. Food was in short supply.

Roosevelt cursed the army's lack of organization. He had been promoted to full colonel and was now even more determined than before to make sure his men had the food they needed. There was a supply of beans available—a half ton of them—he had heard. He would take them for his men, Roosevelt said to the man in charge at the commissary. That couldn't be done, he was told. Those beans were only for the officers.

After some thought Roosevelt walked outside the tent, came back in, and announced that he needed the beans for the regiment's officers. "Colonel," the young sergeant told him, "your officers can't eat eleven hundred pounds of beans."

"You don't know what appetites my officers have," Roosevelt replied and left the commissary with enough food to feed the entire regiment.

After days encamped in the jungle, the men were ordered to move forward to the San Juan Heights, a ridge of hills above the city of Santiago and its harbor. "The jungle formed a wall on either hand," Roosevelt later wrote. The men marched through the midday heat and on into the evening. They waded through a stream, climbed a hill, and camped for the night. At six the next morning, July 1, 1898, as the sun rose into a clear blue sky, the Spanish opened fire on the U.S. encampment. Shells exploded above the troops' heads and bullet shrapnel hit Roosevelt's wrist. Others were not so lucky. A nearby soldier had his leg blown off, and others of the regiment fell dead or wounded.

Roosevelt leaped onto his horse and herded his troops to a protected area of underbrush. Inching their way forward through the thicket in 100-degree heat, the unit emerged at a clearing by the San Juan River, where Spanish bullets and mortars poured down on them. The men waded through the river, which was running red with blood, and swam to the other side.

Some of the men, under furious fire from the Spanish, took refuge in the water or lay in the tall grass. Other U.S. regiments were struggling their way upward. Bullets cut through the air, leaving a trail of dying and injured soldiers in their wake. Nearby, more soldiers, also under heavy fire, began their ascent of the San Juan Heights.

"Bullets drove in sheets through the trees and the tall jungle grass," Roosevelt wrote, "making a peculiar whirring or rustling sound. . . . If a man was shot through the heart, spine or brain he was, of course, killed instantly."

Roosevelt waited impatiently for the command to attack. Then came the order for his unit to move forward and support the regulars. The young colonel mounted his horse and began the adventure that would propel him into international fame. Galloping up Kettle Hill, he cajoled his men to follow. When they hung back, he yelled, "Are you afraid to stand up when I am on horseback?" Surrounded by the dead and wounded, he issued commands to troops whose officers had fallen.

Plunging across a stream, Roosevelt urged his horse farther up the hill. The Spanish had tried to block the way with barbed wire, but members of the all-black 9th Regiment cleared the area. A friend had given Roosevelt a revolver that had been salvaged from the *Maine*, and he aimed it at a Spanish soldier, fired, and saw the man collapse.

As he crested Kettle Hill, he saw the Spanish troops fleeing down the opposite side. In the distance Spanish ships lay in the Santiago harbor. Beyond the mouth of the harbor, the U.S. Navy's squadron floated in wait. U.S. soldiers, under heavy bombardment, were struggling up a nearby hill of the San Juan Heights. They would never make it without help, he thought. The Rough Riders must join them.

Urging his horse forward, he began riding furiously down Kettle Hill. Then, realizing that his troops had not heard his order to follow, he backtracked and gave the command again. Together, the men on foot, and Roosevelt with his blue-and-white bandanna floating behind him in the breeze, charged up the San Juan Heights.

When Roosevelt and the Rough Riders reached the summit of the San Juan Heights, they could see the battle-weary Spaniards retreating toward Santiago. The ground was thick with corpses, but Roosevelt and his men had won the victory. Surely, he thought, he would receive the Medal of Honor, the military's highest tribute for valor in battle.

But the war was not quite over. There was still the matter of the Spanish ships in Santiago Harbor. Now, with Spanish ground soldiers defeated, the U.S. Navy was able to torpedo the Spanish fleet, leaving it totally ruined. Little was left but to negotiate a surrender. Roosevelt, with his supreme belief in the Monroe Doctrine, was about to see the Spanish leave the Western Hemisphere. And he had played a key role in their removal.

Leading troops up the San Juan Heights to defeat the Spanish was a high point in TR's life. The Rough Riders wore blue shirts, wide-brimmed hats, and bandannas knotted around their necks.

Roosevelt took this family photo with him to Cuba. It shows him holding Archie, with Ted standing next to Alice, TR's daughter by his first marriage. Edith, his wife, holds Kermit *(left)* and Ethel.

The U.S. soldiers still had to fight another war, however: the war against disease. Contaminated water, tropical heat, and disease-carrying mosquitoes had taken their toll on the troops as they camped out in the Cuban jungles. Malaria and dysentery felled twice as many men as Spanish bullets. Senior officers restlessly waited for orders from President McKinley and Secretary of War Russell Alger to bring their troops home. The men were sick and becoming sicker. They needed to be in the United States, where they could get the necessary care.

But the order did not come. Roosevelt, encouraged by the other officers, drafted a joint letter to General Shafter, saying that U.S. troops should be taken out of Cuba immediately. If they were not, the letter implied, those in charge of the military would be responsible for more lives lost. Roosevelt added a letter of his own, criticizing the handling of the situation. Then, to cap matters off, the letters were deliberately leaked to the Associated Press and appeared in newspapers all over the United States.

President McKinley was livid when he read the press reports criticizing his administration. Roosevelt might be a hero in Cuba and to the American public, but he certainly wasn't a hero to McKinley or the staff at the War Department in

Washington. An officer in the military did not question orders from his superiors—and certainly not in public. Roosevelt could forget about the Medal of Honor.

The American people, however, were ready to welcome Roosevelt home with open arms. And when the Rough Riders finally disembarked at Montauk Point on New York's Long Island, where they had been sent for quarantine, their leader was greeted with cheers of "Roosevelt, Roosevelt." Roosevelt, tanned and fit, grinned his famous smile from ear to ear. "I will not say a word about myself," Roosevelt told

TR and the Medal of Honor

One of Roosevelt's bitter disappointments was not being awarded the U.S. Medal of Honor. Though he had performed heroically during the Spanish-American War, President McKinley and the War Department did not take kindly to his open criticism of their treatment of U.S. troops suffering from yellow fever. However, more than a hundred years later, on January 16, 2001, Theodore Roosevelt was awarded the Medal of Honor posthumously. At the ceremony President William J. Clinton presented the medal to Roosevelt's great-grandson Tweed Roosevelt in the Roosevelt Room of the White House. Theodore Roosevelt was, Clinton reminded the assembled family members, "a larger-than-life figure who gave our nation a larger-than-life vision of our place in the world."

When Roosevelt returned home from Cuba, he was hailed as a war hero. Even as his unit awaited discharge on Long Island, plans were under way for him to run for governor of New York.

reporters, "but I will talk about the regiment forever." His unit had suffered more casualities than any other, Roosevelt recounted proudly. Those who had survived were devoted to Roosevelt for life.

On one of their last days together, after six weeks of quarantine, the men gathered to present a gift to their leader: a bronze statue sculpted by Frederic Remington, one of America's finest western artists. The figure was an American cowboy astride a bucking bronco. The rider, waving his broad-brimmed sombrero in the air, exhibited the same energy and courage the Rough Riders had exhibited in their weeks of training and battle. Colonel Roosevelt's eyes filled with tears and his voice cracked as he thanked his men.

Years later he wrote, "The future greatness of America in no small degree depends upon . . . the qualities which my men showed when they served under me in Santiago."

Chapter 9

"NEW YORK POLITICS"

The leaves on the trees in upstate New York were turning in the autumn of 1898, and all through the state throngs of people were heading for their local train stations. Colonel Theodore Roosevelt was running on the Republican ticket for governor of New York, touring towns and villages in his special campaign train. It seemed everyone wanted to see the hero of the San Juan Heights. He did not disappoint them.

Roosevelt would lean forward from the platform at the rear of the train and raise his high-pitched voice above the cheering crowd and plead for reform. State officials were corrupt, he would shout. Tammany Hall bosses were still running the Democratic Party—they had kept a qualified judge off the state supreme court just because he wasn't loyal enough to Tammany Hall. It was an outrage, Roosevelt told the crowd, his voice shrill with indignation.

Yes, the man's voice was strange. And his message was nothing new. But Roosevelt sent a thrill through the crowd. There was something about him: his energy, his passion, his call for reform, and the courage he had shown in the Spanish-American War. He would fight for them, his listeners believed. He would stand up for them against the big corporations. He would drive dishonest politicians from the state. He was their man, their hero.

Roosevelt wound up his speeches to the sound of cheering. As the locomotive gained speed, it would chug toward the next rural town, leaving an adoring crowd

After the Spanish-American War, cartoonists began depicting "Teddy" Roosevelt wearing his cowboy hat, rimless spectacles, and famous ear-to-ear grin. This cartoon is by Oscar Cesare.

behind. In the small town of Carthage, hundreds of citizens ran alongside the train, waving and cheering as the figure on the platform receded in the distance.

Theodore Roosevelt was on the campaign trail, and he loved it.

Not everyone in the Republican Party had wanted Roosevelt to head the state's ticket. He was headstrong and independent. Senator Thomas C. Platt, called the Easy Boss, been in charge of New York State politics for years. First he chose the state officials, then he told them what to do. Roosevelt wouldn't stand for that if he was elected governor, Platt surmised. But the current Republican administration was dishonest and the incumbent governor probably could not get reelected. Roosevelt, on the other hand, was both honest and enormously popular. He would surely be elected if he ran. So Boss Platt gave in, and Roosevelt again entered the world of politics.

Roosevelt was a natural campaigner. At rallies members of the Rough Rider regiment, dressed in their uniforms and carrying the American flag, galloped at the head of his entourage. His whistle-stop train tour snaked its way through the state. He traveled thousands of miles during the campaign and made more than one hundred speeches a week. When his voice became so hoarse he couldn't speak, one of the Rough Riders spoke for him.

On the train platform, he would strike a pose so that photographers could capture a great shot. He knew how to talk to reporters, shake hands at a county fair, kiss babies, and listen to factory workers. In short, he knew how to get votes. And, on November 8, 1898, he won enough of them to make him the new governor of New York.

The inaugural parade took place in Albany on January 2, 1899, a day so cold the brass instruments in the marching band froze and wouldn't make a sound. There was only a solemn drumbeat as Roosevelt marched through streets lined with thousands of cheering supporters. At the state capitol he climbed the broad white marble steps and strode down the impressive halls to his new office.

With dignity he entered the assembly chamber where he had begun his political career. Cheers from the legislators greeted him. Edith was there with the children, and his friends from the press were waiting to see how he would begin his term.

In his speech, the young governor called for better working and living conditions for immigrants. Labor laws protecting workers should be strictly enforced, and sweatshops, those "unwholesome, pest-creating, and crime-breeding workshops," should be regularly inspected and forced to comply with licensing. The eight-hour workday for state employees should be honored.

He also touched on one of his favorite causes, conservation. New land could be acquired by the state, but it was important to protect current state reserves from "the depredations of man" as well as one of the "most serious enemies to forests—fire."

And there was the issue of taxes. The current tax system was "in utter confusion" and "full of injustices," he said. He did not go into specifics. He simply asked the legislature to pay special attention to the matter. But the mere mention of tax reform must have made Boss Platt choke. Revising the current tax system could mean making big businesses pay their fair share. Big businesses had always supported the Republican Party with money and with votes. Now, as the new governor began his term in office, it became clear Roosevelt planned to make them ante up.

Streetcars, buses, and power companies in New York State were owned by monopolies, or franchises. Big business raked in enormous profits, in part because they didn't have to pay taxes on the state resources they used. Not fair, Roosevelt declared. If they were using state land, water, pipelines, or other resources, they ought to be charged.

Boss Platt was furious. The new governor had already crossed him once. Right after the election, Platt told Roosevelt that he had chosen a new state superintendent of public works. He had already offered him the position, and the man had said yes. Platt even showed Roosevelt the telegram. But Roosevelt balked. *He* was governor, not Platt. It was *his* place to appoint the superintendent, not Platt's.

On the other hand, Roosevelt needed Platt's support. Perhaps he could find a way to make his own appointment but still allow Platt to save face. Roosevelt made a list of three people he would accept for the job. He told Platt to choose the one he wanted. The Easy Boss wasn't happy about the list—his man wasn't on it. But at least he had a choice: He was the one making the final decision.

It was no wonder that Platt and Roosevelt had trouble working together on tax reform. The two men held entirely different opinions. Platt thought business and politics went together like coffee and cream. Roosevelt thought the combination led to corruption. If a ditch digger had to pay taxes on his paltry wages, then big corporations should have to pay, too. It was only fair, Roosevelt believed.

Pass a bill that would require franchises to pay taxes and he would sign it, Roosevelt told the legislature. If he did, it would be the mistake of his life, Platt told him. New York's businessmen would never support him if he taxed them. He would hurt the party and his own political future. And he, Platt, would do everything to make sure the bill did not pass.

Roosevelt knew that machine politics, run by Platt and his cronies, was a powerful force in the state, and he wanted to accomplish as much as possible in as short a time as he could. "New York politics are kaleidoscopic and 18 months hence I may be so much out of kilter with the machine that there will be no possibility of my renomination," he wrote to his friend Henry Cabot Lodge in April 1899. For help in gaining support for his programs, he turned to the press.

Each morning Governor Roosevelt opened the door to his executive office and greeted reporters from all over the state. Then for fifteen minutes he perched on the edge of his mahogany desk to chat. He told reporters how he felt about bills on the floor of the assembly and confided his plans for the future. Each afternoon, the

As governor of New York, Roosevelt met daily with reporters. Later, on his first day as president, he met with the heads of the three major news services, establishing good communications with the press early on in his administration.

press was back again while Roosevelt briefed them on what had happened during the morning session. He was charming, witty, and informative. When the press needed a good story, Roosevelt provided one. And when Roosevelt needed information he couldn't get any other way, he asked the reporters to find out for him.

Right now he needed information on the tax bill. How many votes did he have in the assembly, he asked the reporters. Enough to pass it, they responded. Roosevelt was jubilant. He'd taken on big business and Boss Platt, and he had won.

Platt wasn't happy about the tax on franchises. Nor was he happy about Roosevelt's relationship with labor leaders. Unions had a bad name with wealthy business owners. Strikes often turned ugly, as workers rioted in hopes of forcing better wages and working conditions. Employers brought in armed guards, and state militia marched on the workers, shooting and clubbing the crowds. During the 1890s several violent worker riots struck terror into the hearts of the rich and middle class.

These workers must be communists, anarchists, or terrorists, many Americans thought. Some were. Most, however, were just poor immigrants fed up with their horrible conditions. They had no health insurance, no savings, no time off, no sick leave, no vacation. They often were at their jobs for fourteen hours a day, six days a week. They received less than ten dollars a week and lived in crowded, unsanitary tenements. Meanwhile, their bosses lived in elaborate mansions, rode in fancy carriages, and ate at expensive restaurants. When the unions promised the workers a better deal, they signed up.

Roosevelt hated anarchists. They were un-American—the worst of sins, in his mind. And he had no use for the violence that often came with the struggle for workers' rights. Fighting in Cuba was one thing; fighting on the picket line was another. But he had learned about workers' conditions when he had served as an assemblyman and as police commissioner in New York City. He knew the United States didn't treat all its citizens equally. His own children played freely and happily at Oyster Bay, while tenement children spent their days in cramped, dirty spaces. His wife could be with her family, while immigrant mothers labored all day in factories, away from their children. Often even the children had to work in the factories to help make ends meet.

Roosevelt did not expect everyone in America to be rich. But he did believe that the poor should have better working and living conditions. He met with labor leaders and listened to their concerns. Platt and Republican businessmen disapproved of the governor having anything to do with labor.

They also disapproved when Roosevelt set out to reform the state's department of forestry. The state owned thousands of acres of land rich with ancient trees and wildlife, but they were poorly managed. Roosevelt had become good friends with Gifford Pinchot, the head of the agency that became the U.S. Forest Service. Together the two mapped out a plan for protecting New York from lumbermen who made fortunes clearing timber on state lands.

Songbirds, those lovely creatures Roosevelt knew so well from his days in the woods, were disappearing at an alarming rate. Manufacturers killed them by the thousands just for their feathers, which were then used to decorate expensive hats and dresses. There should be laws, Roosevelt believed, to protect the state's natural resources from greedy businessmen.

New York State's businessmen and Boss Platt were beginning to realize that

Overcrowding, poor health conditions, child labor, and brutally long hours were standard fare for many New York City workers. As a state assemblyman, as governor, and later as president, Roosevelt pushed government to provide better conditions for American workers.

Roosevelt would be a thorn in their sides as long as he was governor. They were probably relieved when the Roosevelts left Albany for a few days to travel to Las Vegas, New Mexico, where the Rough Riders were gathering for a reunion. They were not pleased, however, when they learned of the cheering crowds that turned out for Roosevelt at every train stop. He was a hero. It was almost as if he were running for president. It was time, they agreed, for the famous Rough Rider to be reigned in.

When Roosevelt arrived back in Albany he was greeted by a scandal that was about to become public. The state insurance inspector had been involved in shady dealings with the very industry he was supposed to regulate. He had violated the public trust. The man must go, Roosevelt declared. No, said Platt, he'll stay. Roosevelt stuck to his guns, and the man left.

Platt realized there was no way to control the brash, reform-minded governor. He decided that Roosevelt should leave the governorship. And he had a plan.

Chapter 10

"A MOST HONORABLE OFFICE"

Thomas Platt thought he had just the job for Theodore Roosevelt—vice president of the United States. President McKinley's vice president, Garret Hobart, had died in late November 1899, and the president needed a running mate in the 1900 election. Platt began to scheme. If he could convince Republican Party leaders that Roosevelt was a strong candidate for the empty slot, the energetic governor would be out of New York State politics.

The popular young reformer could not do much harm in the vice president's office, Platt reasoned. It *sounded* like an important job, but everyone knew that vice presidents did not have any real power. They just presided over the Senate, made a few speeches, and attended ceremonial events. Perfect, Platt thought.

Roosevelt's friend, Senator Henry Cabot Lodge, also encouraged him to run for vice president. His motivation was different from Platt's, though. Lodge thought Roosevelt would make a good presidential candidate in 1904.

There was just one problem: Roosevelt didn't want the job. In a letter to Lodge he protested that "the Vice-Presidency is a most honorable office, but for a young man there is not much to do." To his sister Bamie he wrote definitively, "I do not want the vice-presidency." He would rather be governor of New York for another term, or governor-general of the Philippines, or perhaps secretary of war in Washington.

Edith didn't like the idea, either. If her husband became vice president, the family would have to live in Washington and she and the children would have less time with him. And what about money? The vice president was paid less than the governor of New York. With six children and expensive tastes, the Roosevelts needed more income.

But Platt and his cohorts continued their scheming. On the one hand, Platt advised Roosevelt against thinking about the vice presidency. He would be "simply shelved," and unable to do anything significant. At the same time, though, Platt was consulting with other party leaders about putting Roosevelt's name in nomination. Not all of them agreed with the Boss's plan. Mark Hanna, the wealthy Ohio industrialist who had plotted, planned, and paid for William McKinley's campaign, was appalled. "Don't you realize," he said, "that if Roosevelt becomes vice president there is only one man between that mad man and the presidency?"

In December 1899 Roosevelt wrote to Lodge again. "I find that after Platt's return from Washington he *did* tell a couple of New York politicians that I would undoubtedly have to accept the Vice-Presidency, that events were shaping themselves so that this was inevitable. He gave me no hint of this, taking exactly the opposite view...and I do not understand what is up."

In June 1900 Republican delegates gathered in Philadelphia to choose the nominees for the upcoming election. Henry Cabot Lodge, who was chairman of the convention, had repeatedly told Roosevelt he planned to nominate him for vice president. Roosevelt continued to tell him he did not want to run.

But it was not Roosevelt's decision. Platt had made it obvious that he would try to block Roosevelt from returning to Albany as governor, no matter how much he wanted the job. And when Roosevelt appeared at the Republican convention in Philadelphia, he was flattered by the groundswell of support for his nomination.

Mark Hanna, the president's close adviser, continued to oppose a McKinley-Roosevelt ticket. Roosevelt could not be controlled, he feared. McKinley, though, remained neutral, refusing to endorse any candidate. He said that the decision was up to the delegates at the convention. Finally, after much backroom dealing, Hanna lent his support to Roosevelt.

By this time Roosevelt was buoyed by the lively, flag-waving demonstrations in his favor. He and Lodge, representing the independent wing of the Republican

As candidate for vice president, Roosevelt traveled the country for the Republican ticket. Meanwhile, President William McKinley sat out the campaign on his porch in Ohio.

Party, were the heroes of the convention. He seconded the nomination of President McKinley and delivered a stirring speech. On June 21, 1900, he was nominated to be McKinley's running mate for vice president in the fall election.

Roosevelt voted against himself, but once he had done so and the rest of the delegates had enthusiastically put him on the national ticket, he plunged whole-heartedly into the campaign. While McKinley ran for reelection sitting in a rocking chair on his front porch in Canton, Ohio, Roosevelt swept across the country, rounding up votes for the Republican ticket.

Shown here in Bangor, Maine, TR took his ideas for a more powerful government to the people, drawing thousands of listeners whenever he spoke.

For weeks he crisscrossed the United States by train, the Rough Riders leading his parades. William Jennings Bryan, who had lost to McKinley in 1896, was running again on the Democratic ticket. He was a spellbinding speaker, and he appealed to farmers and laborers, who wanted a president who paid more attention to their concerns.

But Roosevelt could speak for the workers, too. He believed in reform. He would stand up to big business, he told voters. It almost seemed that Roosevelt, not McKinley, was running against Bryan. In the end, Bryan was no match for Roosevelt's enthusiasm and popularity. On November 6, 1900, McKinley and Roosevelt swept the country, winning the election by a wide margin.

In Albany, Edith began organizing the bikes, skates, clothes, and pets that the children had accumulated during their two years' stay in the governor's mansion. A new century was just beginning, and Theodore Roosevelt was leaving his home state for the nation's capital.

He had packed several lifetimes of adventure and action into his forty-two years: state assemblyman, rancher, husband, father of six, big-game hunter; expert on birds and mammals; author; civil service commissioner; New York City police commissioner; assistant secretary of the U.S. Navy; war hero; and governor of New York.

Now he was vice president of the United States, a job without the power and challenges that he thrived on. He had big ambitions for America and longed to put them into action. But right now he was only vice president. For now he must learn to be content with that.

Chapter 11

"I FELT AT ONCE THAT HE HAD BAD NEWS"

Roosevelt was right. The vice presidency was not the ideal job for him. He wanted more responsibility, more activity. President McKinley and his adviser Mark Hanna wanted Roosevelt to stay in the background and avoid the limelight. They thought he was "indiscreet and over impulsive," Roosevelt confided to a friend.

In the ornate, wood-paneled chambers of Congress, he lifted his gavel, brought it down with a crack, and began his duties presiding over the Senate. Sitting behind the podium in a large leather armchair, he wondered how he would spend the rest of the year. He had been sworn into office on March 4, 1901, the day then used for presidential inaugurations. But Congress had decided to adjourn on March 8 and not reconvene until December. That left Roosevelt with a lot of free time.

Perhaps he would take up the study of the law again and finish the degree he had begun years before. Or he might write another book. He had published thirteen by now. He had dictated the last one to a stenographer while he was governor, amazing his staff with his ability to switch between delivering a steady stream of historic information and doing the necessary duties of running the state.

He would, of course, spend time with Edith and the children. That was always a pleasant prospect. Oyster Bay and Sagamore Hill were lovely in the summer. There the family would row across the Sound, picnic, bird watch, and read. He could also travel and take a couple of trips out west. And there were some ceremonial duties that the vice president had to perform that would keep him busy until Congress reconvened.

There was, for instance, the opening of the Pan-American Exposition. In late May he and Edith traveled from Oyster Bay to Buffalo, where Roosevelt presided over the opening of the exhibits and gave a speech. In the summer he traveled west. Then, as summer turned to early fall, the Roosevelts headed for a family vacation in the Adirondack Mountains. Theodore took a side trip to Vermont to make a speech and visit the state's former governor, Nelson W. Fisk. It looked as if the next three and a half years were going to be pretty dull for an ambitious man like Roosevelt.

Meanwhile, President McKinley and his wife left Washington, D.C., and headed north by train to Buffalo to visit the Pan-American Exposition that the vice president had opened a few months earlier. On September 6, 1901, while Roosevelt was attending a reception for Fisk, President McKinley stepped into the Temple of Music on the Exposition grounds and made his way through the potted palms, shaking hands with the people crowding the hall. Thousands of supporters had turned out to greet McKinley and his wife. He was a popular president, and this was his first visit to the city since he had been reelected.

Two years earlier the men assigned to protect the president had worried about crowds like this. Anarchists had made attacks in the United States and elsewhere in the world, and guards had been on high alert. This year, though, things seemed quieter. Security was a little looser even as the crowds pressed across the roped-off areas to shake the president's hand.

McKinley leaned forward to greet a young man wearing a bandage on his right hand. Suddenly, there was the sound of a gunshot. The president doubled over and fell to the ground. The bandage on the man's hand was no bandage—it was a handkerchief concealing a revolver, which the angry anarchist had used to pump bullets into the president's stomach and chest. Secret Service agents leaped on the assassin. McKinley was rushed to a local hospital, where he lay in grave condition, close to death.

In Vermont, Vice President Roosevelt was chatting with companions at the reception for Fisk. He was interrupted by a phone call telling him the news, which

Anarchists who sought to overthrow the government were often associated with the violent riots and strikes of the late 1800s. In this artist's depiction, an anarchist shoots President McKinley with a concealed revolver at the Pan-American Exposition reception.

left him shocked and furious. The attack on the president was a "blow at America's essence," he said. Taking the next train to Buffalo, Roosevelt hurried to McKinley's side.

For three days surgeons in Buffalo labored around the clock to keep the president alive. Finally, his fever fell and his ashen face regained some of its healthier color. He was on the mend, his doctors believed, and Roosevelt left to rejoin Edith and the children in the Adirondacks. It had been a close call. Roosevelt had almost become president. Now, though, he was free to go for a hike and climb a nearby mountain.

With a couple of climbing companions, Roosevelt set out in the rain to hike up the rigorous path leading to the top of Mount Marcy. They reached the summit shortly before noon, then headed back toward the cabin where he and his family were staying. Halfway down the mountain, the group stopped for lunch by a lake. As they were eating, a guide came toward them from the woods.

After McKinley was assassinated in Buffalo, New York, Roosevelt *(left)* hurried there to be sworn in as president. Mark Hanna, McKinley's closest adviser (in white hat), distrusted Roosevelt and called him "that damned cowboy."

"I felt at once that he had bad news," Roosevelt wrote later. The president had taken a turn for the worse. Later in the day a second telegram arrived. The president was dying. Roosevelt must come at once.

The road was treacherously slick with mud as Roosevelt and a lone wagon driver made their way down the dark twisty path to the nearest train station. It was almost dawn before they reached tiny North Creek, where McKinley's secretary was waiting for them. After appearing to be on the mend, the president had developed an infection that the doctors could not treat, and he had died early that morning. Hurriedly Roosevelt boarded the train and sped through the night.

At approximately three-thirty on the afternoon of September 14, 1901, a small group gathered in the living room of the Buffalo home of Ansley Wilcox, a friend of Roosevelt's. Cabinet members and other dignitaries waited for the vice president to enter the room. He had arrived in Buffalo still wearing his camping gear. Now, dressed in a borrowed formal shirt, coat, and striped pants, he asked that reporters be allowed into the room to witness his swearing in. Then he turned to face federal judge John Hazel. Placing his left hand on a borrowed Bible, he raised his right hand and took the presidential oath of office, promising to uphold the Constitution of the United States.

At age forty-two he became the twenty-sixth president of the United States. He was the youngest man ever to hold that honor.

Chapter 12

"A HOUSEHOLD OF CHILDREN"

The Roosevelt children were at it again. Ever since they had moved into the Executive Mansion in Washington, they had been tearing through its hallways looking for more ways to get into trouble. The two youngest boys roller-skated in the basement and stalked on their stilts through the stately reception rooms. They discovered metal trays in the kitchen—and then used them as slides for clattering noisily down the main staircase. Quentin and his friends startled visitors by popping out of the tall decorative vases that stood in the East Room.

At the breakfast table, while his father had his usual bowl of peaches and cream, Kermit insisted on feeding lumps of sugar to his kangaroo rat, one of the many Roosevelt pets that had taken up residence in the Executive Mansion. There was a kitten who nipped the ankles of visiting dignitaries, a macaw, a badger named Josiah, two ponies, and Alice's emerald green snake named Emily Spinach.

The Roosevelt children were boisterous and needed room, but their new home was stiff and formal. And it was too small. Both the family bedrooms and the executive offices for the president were located on the second floor, separated only by a screen at the end of the hallway. It was a good thing that Ted, the eldest, was off at boarding school in Groton, Massachusetts, because there simply wasn't enough room for all six of the Roosevelt children, their parents, and the various guests who visited. And the house was badly out of date. The plumbing was worn out and the electrical wiring was dangerous. Mice and rats scurried in the walls.

The American public was intrigued by the six rambunctious Roosevelt children and their pets, such as Archie's dog and Ted's parrot.

Together Edith and Theodore set out to make some changes. The Executive Mansion would now officially be called the White House, the president announced. And it must be made more gracious and accommodating. Edith ordered fresh flowers for the downstairs reception rooms and arranged the family's collections of books on the shelves. Congress appropriated money to renovate the presidential residence.

Armed with architects' plans approved by the first lady, carpenters, plumbers, electricians, and decorators swung into action. For months they sawed, hammered, wired, draped, and upholstered, while the Roosevelts stayed across the street and then enjoyed a long summer at Oyster Bay. There was a new addition to the White House now, the West Wing, where the president and his aides would have their offices. And there was more room upstairs in the family living quarters.

Theodore was getting too portly, Edith thought, because he went to so many state dinners. He did not get enough exercise. What he needed was a tennis court, so she had one built just outside his office. The president loved tennis and at one time had played ninety-six games back-to-back at Oyster Bay. Now the new court became a regular gathering spot for Roosevelt's "tennis cabinet," a collection of close friends and government officials. But it didn't do anything to reduce his weight. He was too busy to exercise as much as he once had. But he always found time to read. Edith had arranged for him to have a den upstairs in the family quarters, and almost every night he was still awake reading a book at midnight or one o'clock.

For the youngest Roosevelts, the newly renovated White House was an expanded playground. Delighted with the new East Room, Archie and Quentin immediately claimed it as a roller rink, leaving skate marks on the polished parquet floors. And when Archie lay sick in bed and needed cheering up, Quentin smuggled Algonquin, his brother's favorite pony, onto the elevator and up into his brother's bedroom. Theodore "thinks children should be given entire freedom for their own inclinations," Edith told a friend.

The gloomy old White House was full of life now that TR and his exuberant crew were in residence. Alice was seventeen years old and a breathtaking beauty. And she was a handful. She flirted with boys, smoked, went to the racetrack, defied her parents, and stayed out late. "I can be president of the United States, or I can attend to Alice," Roosevelt said. But he could not do both.

When it came time for Alice's debut—a lavish ball in honor of her eighteenth birthday—she sulked about the plans for the party. The old furniture in the White House was ugly and out of date, she complained. Washington was so stodgy. In New York her friends served champagne and gave expensive favors like gold watches and silver cigarette cases to their guests, but mother had nixed both ideas. What a bore. There would be no champagne, only punch. And no lavish gifts.

Despite Alice's complaints, the ball was a success. She was surrounded by

Quentin *(far right)* and Archie, shown here with the White House police, terrorized state visitors by popping out of potted plant containers and riding their bikes through the stately rooms of the executive mansion.

ambassadors and a throng of rich, handsome men, including her distant cousin, Franklin Delano Roosevelt. Aunt Corinne, her father's sister, later wrote: "Alice had the time of her life, men seven deep around her all the time," and the party went on till two in the morning.

But Washington was not young Alice's favorite place. New York and Newport, where her wealthier, more sophisticated friends gathered, were more her style, and she spent much of her time away from the White House. There were advantages, though, to being the president's daughter. A visiting prince from Germany was so taken with her that he asked her to christen his new yacht, then gave her a diamond bracelet.

Alice's younger brother Ted was in school at Groton, where he had made the football team. That was just the kind of news his father liked to hear. But later the president learned that Ted had broken his collarbone in a game. Next he permanently damaged one of his front teeth. "Ted would have a fit if he knew I were

Roosevelt wrote more than 150,000 letters, many of them to his children. Here, in what he called a "picture letter," he writes to Ethel and illustrates various family goings-on.

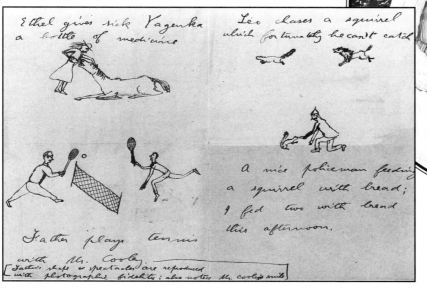

Ethel gives sick Vagenka a bottle of medicine

Leo chases a squirrel which fortunately he can't catch

A nice policeman feeding a squirrel with bread; I fed two with bread this afternoon.

Father plays tennis with Mr. Cooley.
[Father's shape & spectacles are reproduced with photographic fidelity; also notice Mr. Cooley's smile]

There! My invention has given out! Mother & Aunt Emily have been on a picnic down the river with several cousins; we have been sitting on the portico in the moonlight. Sister is very good.
Your loving father

WHITE HOUSE. WASHINGTON June 22d 1904
Darling Ethel,
Here goes for the picture letter!

Ethel administers necessary discipline to Archie and Quentin.

"There could be no healthier and pleasanter place in which to bring up children," TR wrote of Sagamore Hill, the Roosevelt family home on Long Island. He led his children on hikes, played ball with them, and told ghost stories around campfires.

writing..." the president said in a letter to the school's headmaster. He hated to ask for special treatment for his son, but, he pointed out, his son was only fourteen years old and if he continued to be roughed up in football, he would not be able to play in college.

When his father had been civil service commissioner, his son Ted often walked to the office with him. "On the way down he would talk history to me," Ted Jr. remembered as an adult. "Not the dry history of dates and charters, but the history where you yourself in your imagination could assume the role of the principal actors.... During every battle we would stop and father would draw out the full plan in the dust in the gutter with the tip of his umbrella."

Now that Roosevelt was president he still found time to spend with his children and be a good father. When he recalled his days in the White House years later, he wrote, "For unflagging interest and enjoyment, a household of children... certainly makes all other forms of success and achievement lose their importance by comparison."

Chapter 13

"NO EASY JOB"

While the children romped and Edith entertained friends and heads of state, Theodore was learning about his new job. "It is no easy job being President," he wrote to his son Ted in October 1901, "but I am thoroughly enjoying it and I think so far I have done pretty well."

He had promised the leaders of the Republican Party that he would not do anything rash. He would move slowly and maintain the country's prosperity. But two of his early actions filled his critics with dread.

In 1901 the United States was still a segregated country, and American Negroes and whites didn't socialize. But Roosevelt admired Booker T. Washington, a prominent Negro educator and leader who had established the Tuskegee Institute in Alabama. Roosevelt frequently consulted him on political appointments in the South. The president, Washington believed, "wanted to help not only the Negro, but the whole South."

In mid-October, soon after he had taken office, Roosevelt invited Booker T. Washington to dine with him at the White House. Blacks had come to the White House before, but none had ever been invited to dinner with the president. When the press reported on the guest list, the South was up in arms.

In a barrage of racial slurs, southern newspapers and politicians attacked Roosevelt. The invitation was, one publisher declared, "the most damnable outrage ever." Another newspaper wrote that Roosevelt must believe "there is no racial

ABOVE: When Roosevelt invited Booker T. Washington (*seated next to Roosevelt*) to the White House for dinner, southern newspapers lambasted the president.

LEFT: The *Cleveland Gazette*, an African American newspaper, worried that Roosevelt's invitation to Booker T. Washington would create a backlash by whites against blacks.

We very much fear that President Roosevelt's entertainment of Booker T. Washington, while perfectly right and proper, will eventually prove the latter's undoing, as far as his great educational work is concerned. The prejudiced southern white people are vindictive and will punish some one for the social distinction conferred upon Mr. Washington and the race by the president. They are now trying to vent their spleen upon our entire race and the president through the medium of the southern press and its northern prejudiced sympathizers, and will not be satisfied with the results. Privately, or rather sectionally, they will quietly work upon Washington and his great school. Some years will elapse before the effect will be noticed in a general way. This is to be regretted as much as the president's action in inviting an Afro-American to dine and counsel with him is to be commended.

reason . . . why whites and blacks may not marry." Did Roosevelt think blacks were equal with whites, the critics asked? If the president of the United States invited blacks to the White House, who knew what might happen next! If blacks could be invited to the White House, they might start thinking they could intermingle socially with whites. It was outrageous—a scandal.

Roosevelt tried to explain. He was simply "showing some little respect to a man whom I cordially esteem as a good citizen and a good American," he said. The president had been unprepared for the public response, and he was saddened by the racial hatred that still existed in America. He continued to consult with Washington, but there were no more dinner invitations for Washington or any other blacks during his presidency.

Roosevelt's next move caused outrage in the business community. J. P. Morgan was one of the richest and most powerful men in America. He had made a fortune as a New York banker and had financed many of the country's industries. He made loans to dig coal mines, build steel mills, construct oil rigs, and lay the rails for the country's ever-expanding train system. American industry depended on Morgan and his money. He had bailed out the nation during an economic crash in 1895. He had contributed to Roosevelt's campaign when he ran for governor of New York, and he expected the government to leave his businesses alone.

Roosevelt knew the United States would never be a major world power without industry. In his first message to Congress he praised large corporations for their contributions to the nation. "The captains of industry who have driven the railway systems across this continent, who have built up our commerce, who have developed our manufacturers, have on the whole done great good to our people," he said.

But, he warned, the new century brought new challenges. Cities and industries had expanded so rapidly that the old laws regulating business no longer worked. Family business owners used to take care of their workers and their customers. Now those days were gone. Huge, impersonal corporations had taken their place.

Sometimes big business went too far, Roosevelt thought. And he felt that J. P. Morgan had gone too far when he set out to form the Northern Securities Company. Morgan planned to combine several rail lines into one giant trust, or monopoly. With Morgan's money the trust could lower prices enough to put smaller competitors out of business. Then farmers and ranchers would not have their choice of shippers to get their goods to market. Once Morgan formed his monopoly, the trust could raise prices as high as it wanted.

Roosevelt remembered his days in the West and the men and women there who eked out a living raising and selling livestock. It was a hard life and every penny counted. They needed protection from unscrupulous businessmen. The Northern Securities Company was anticompetitive, Roosevelt decided. It violated the Sherman Antitrust Act of 1890. The government must oppose the merger, Roosevelt told his attorney general. Bring a U.S. government suit against the Northern Securities Company, he commanded in February 1902.

Morgan was flabbergasted. He had never quite trusted Roosevelt, and like many others he thought the young president was unpredictable. But he had never dreamed that Roosevelt would take such a bold step. "If we have done something wrong, send your man to my man and they can fix it up," he suggested. That was the way wealthy gentlemen did business.

But Roosevelt didn't give an inch and became known as a "trust buster" as he set out to impose government regulations on large business conglomerates. The government must protect all its citizens, he believed, no matter how rich or poor they were. And small businesses must be protected from unfair competition. "Men of wealth must play by the rules," he said. Roosevelt was right in opposing the Northern Securities merger, the Supreme Court later ruled in 1904. Morgan's plans for a railroad trust violated the U.S. Constitution and the Sherman Antitrust Act, and the company must be dissolved.

"Busting trusts" was serious business, but Roosevelt couldn't stay serious for long. In his White House office he happily greeted a steady stream of daily visitors. In the mornings, after he had gone for a walk and answered his mail, the room filled up with congressmen, cabinet members, and dozens of visitors lobbying for their various causes.

Lincoln Steffens, his friend and a reporter, wrote: "His offices were crowded with people, mostly reformers, all day long, and the President did his work among them with little privacy and much rejoicing. He strode triumphant around among us, talking and shaking hands, dictating and signing letters, and laughing."

Oil, railroad, and banking monopolies assumed they could influence politics and government with their wealth before Roosevelt set out to break up their trusts. Here he is shown as David out to slay the Goliaths of Wall Street.

On a 1902 Mississippi hunting trip Roosevelt refused to shoot an old bear that had been tied to a tree. By 1903, stores were flooded with stuffed "Teddy bears" honoring Roosevelt's good sportsmanship. Clifford Berryman helped make the bears popular through his cartoons.

The afternoons were just as lively. Every day after lunch Roosevelt met with reporters, bantering with them, feeding them news items, and gossiping about government officials. Never one to waste a minute, he arranged for his barber to shave him during his meetings with the press. Often, just as the barber was about to lower the open blade to scrape away at Roosevelt's beard, the president would leap from his seat and wave his arms as he gave an answer to a reporter's question. No president had ever spent so much time with the press, and stories poured from the White House onto the front pages of the country's newspapers.

Sessions with Roosevelt were always fun. "A hundred times a day the President will laugh," a reporter for the *New York Times* wrote. "And when he laughs he does it with the same energy with which he talks. It is usually a roar of laughter, and it comes nearly every five minutes. His face grows red with merriment, his eyes nearly close, his utterance becomes choked and sputtery and falsetto, and sometimes he doubles up in paroxysm. You don't smile with Mr. Roosevelt; you shout with laughter with him, and then you shout again while he tries to cork up more laughter and sputters: 'Come gentlemen, let us be serious.'"

"That damned cowboy," Mark Hanna called Roosevelt in disgust. But the cowboy was in the saddle again. Only this time he was running the country instead of cattle on the range. And he was having the time of his life.

Chapter 14

"A COAL FAMINE"

While the Roosevelt children raced their bikes through the streets of Washington and across the well-tended White House lawn, children elsewhere in America were not as carefree. In the coalfields of Pennsylvania, for instance, twelve-year-old boys spent their days in pitch-black tunnels hundreds of feet beneath the earth's surface. They were helping to mine coal, and their childhood was cut short by the dangerous work they performed.

Their younger brothers who were not old enough yet to go into the mines worked as breaker boys, sitting for hours in front of dusty conveyor belts, sorting lumps of coal according to their size. Their fingers bled, and their lungs filled with coal dust. Their fathers, many of them immigrants from Poland, Wales, Scotland, and Ireland worked down in the mines with the older boys. They were underground for as long as fourteen hours a day.

Together these men and boys mined coal. And in 1902 America ran on coal. Coal fueled trains, ships, and factories. It heated homes and was used in the making of steel. It warmed offices, churches, and schools. Without coal the country would come to a standstill. There would be no heat in winter, no power for the factories, no goods in the stores, no new bridges, no new rail lines, and none of the new automobiles that were becoming so popular.

Mine owners made fortunes from the country's ravenous appetite for the fuel, but the miners did not share in the wealth. The operators owned the mines; they owned the houses the miners lived in and the stores where they shopped. Prices were high and wages were low.

Many miners were crippled or killed in accidents. Coal dust ravaged their lungs, and the steady blasting of dynamite ruined their hearing. And they earned only a few dollars a week. For all the grueling, dangerous hours they spent in the mines, most of them received about $250 a year.

Miners wanted higher wages, shorter hours, and safer working conditions. And they were willing to fight for their demands. The United Mine Workers of America, the largest and strongest labor union in the country, promised miners that they would have more power against the operators if they protested as a group. If they joined together, they could walk off their jobs and close the mines. The public would have to pay attention when there was no coal and the nation came to a standstill.

Early in the spring of 1902, only a few months after Roosevelt had taken office, the United Mine Workers called for a strike. It was not an easy decision for the miners. They had families to feed, and if they walked off their jobs, they would be without paychecks. The union provided some strike pay, but it wasn't much. And once the strike was settled, the operators might blackball the strikers and keep them from getting their old jobs back. There were plenty of new immigrants coming to America who wanted jobs, even jobs in the mines. No, it wouldn't be easy going out on strike. But things weren't getting any better. They had to do something.

On a May morning the whistles that signaled the beginning of the work shift sounded in dozens of coal-mining towns throughout Pennsylvania. But the men who walked out their front doors weren't dressed for work. Leaving their lunch pails and coveralls behind, more than 140,000 anthracite coal miners walked off their jobs. The nation's mines were closed, and the coal strike of 1902 had begun.

Sitting at his desk in Washington, President Roosevelt sensed that he was facing a tremendous challenge. Officially, he had no power to intervene in the strike. It was a matter to be settled by the operators and the union. But the operators refused to recognize the union. As far as the mine owners were concerned, the union didn't even exist. For now all Roosevelt could do was watch and wait.

As the strike continued through the fall, the nation began to feel the effects of going without coal. In the White House, Roosevelt worried about the effects the walkout would have on the nation. "A coal famine in the winter is an awful ugly thing, and I fear we shall see terrible suffering and grave disaster," he wrote to Senator Hanna in early October.

Prices for what coal was available quadrupled. Afraid of facing the winter cold with no heat, desperate men highjacked carloads of the fuel as freight trains passed through their towns. The cold blasts of winter would arrive soon, and there was little coal to heat homes, offices, and schools. The mayor of New York City was worried about the residents of his city and pleaded with Roosevelt. Send in federal troops to settle the strike, he urged.

Sending in federal troops was the last thing Roosevelt wanted to do. The National Guard had been used before to quell labor unrest, and the troops had left

The coal strike of 1902 threatened to cripple the nation until Roosevelt *(far left)* brought labor and mine owners together to settle their differences.

a wake of bitterness. Workers had been shot and killed. Roosevelt was not about to risk such a disaster in his first months as president. But something had to be done.

The least he could do, Roosevelt decided, was get the opposing sides together for a meeting. Reluctantly, seven coal operators showed up at the White House on October 3, 1902. Roosevelt was there, confined to a chair because he had seriously injured his leg when the carriage he was riding in had overturned. (It was an injury that would plague him the rest of his life.) John Mitchell, the head of the United Mine Workers of America, was the only representative of the miners.

Perhaps a tribunal could be formed, Mitchell suggested, including representatives from the miners, the operators, and a neutral party. The miners would abide by whatever decision the three came up with, the union leader promised.

Then the operators spoke. What right did Roosevelt have to expect them to negotiate with the union? The miners were nothing but a bunch of anarchists and outlaws. The president should have sent the military in long ago to drive the miners back to work, they argued.

Roosevelt left the meeting disgusted by the operators' attitude of superiority. "Only one man behaved as a gentleman," Roosevelt wrote in a letter to a friend after the meeting. The one man was John Mitchell. Even Roosevelt had lost his temper.

A few days later the operators showed their arrogance once again. "The rights and interests of the laboring man will be protected and cared for—not by the labor agitators—but by the Christian men to whom God in His infinite wisdom has given the control of the property interests of the country," one of the coal operators told a reporter. When his remarks were published in newspapers throughout the country, many Americans began to side with the miners.

As the strike dragged on, even the coal bosses began to feel the pinch. Without coal to sell, their companies were losing money. It was clear that Roosevelt was not going to help them by bringing in federal troops to crush the union. However, Roosevelt hinted, he might ask federal troops to take over the mines from the owners and operate them in the public interest. That mere threat sent the operators hurrying to the bargaining table. Now they were ready to work out a compromise.

How about arbitration, Roosevelt suggested—how about a panel of experts who would listen to both sides, study the situation, and recommend a solution? Fine, the operators agreed, but they must control who was on the panel. For days Roosevelt and his advisers offered alternatives and compromises. The panel, as structured by the group, called for one labor representative. No, the operators said. They'd already gone far enough in agreeing to arbitration and meeting with Mitchell. Well, Roosevelt suggested, let's not call him a labor representative. We'll call him a "sociologist." The operators consented. They could accept that.

So while the panel did its work, the miners returned to the mines, saved the country from freezing, and got the nation's industries up and running again. When the panel made its recommendation, the miners received a ten percent pay raise and the operators could still refuse to recognize the union. The crisis was over and business returned to normal.

The nation and President Roosevelt breathed a sigh of relief. The new leader had met his first big challenge and had come out a winner. He had his critics, but the American public was growing fonder and fonder of its cowboy president.

Chapter 15

"ROOSEVELT'S COROLLARY"

Theodore Roosevelt was angry. German and British warships were anchored just outside Venezuela's main harbor, bombarding its seaports. European nations had no right to be there, Roosevelt believed, and he planned to make sure they left.

The warships were there because Germany and Great Britain had lent large amounts of money to the government of Venezuela. But now, in 1902, Venezuela refused to repay the loans. So the two European nations were threatening to invade the Latin American nation.

Roosevelt watched warily as the situation unfolded. He was not too worried about Great Britain. That country had become an ally of the United States. But German Kaiser Wilhelm II was unpredictable, and he had a powerful navy. And when the Germans and British landed troops in Venezuela, Roosevelt knew it was time to act. The last thing the United States needed was Germany's presence in the nearby waters of the Caribbean.

Messages were sent in code and kept confidential. Years later, though, Roosevelt wrote that Germany planned to seize part of Venezuela and intervene in running the country. In December 1902 Roosevelt called in the German ambassador to the United States. Admiral Dewey had a squadron of U.S. ships in the Caribbean, Roosevelt warned the ambassador. He could sail for Venezuela in ten days if the Germans did not agree to settle the dispute.

A week went by. There was no response from the Germans. Roosevelt called

Puck, a popular magazine, showed the country's confidence in its new president with this this cover illustration.

again for the German ambassador. Was his country ready to arbitrate, the president asked. The ambassador's response was vague. Then Admiral Dewey would proceed to Venezuela immediately, Roosevelt told him.

A day later the ambassador was back. The Germans were willing to talk now, he told the president. Roosevelt's threat of U.S. naval intervention had worked. Germany even asked if Roosevelt would conduct the negotiations. The president was flattered. Clearly, he had gained a reputation as an important global leader. But there was a new International Court in The Hague in the Netherlands, he pointed out. That was the proper place for the mediation, he suggested diplomatically.

Years later some historians wondered if the events had really happened the way Roosevelt remembered them. But new documents back up his claims. Roosevelt had upheld his passionate belief in the Monroe Doctrine, just the way he recounted it years later.

Over the next several months Roosevelt began to expand that doctrine. By the spring of 1904 European countries were again stirring up things in the Western Hemisphere, where, Roosevelt thought, they had no right to be. An Italian cruiser was floating offshore near the Dominican Republic. France and Germany were involved, too, in an attempt to collect on unpaid loans they had made to the impoverished republic. The disorganized, desperate Dominican government turned to Washington for help. Save us from our creditors, the Dominican officials pleaded.

Roosevelt did not want to annex the country as a U.S. protectorate. Instead, in his annual message to Congress in 1904, he laid out the basic philosophy of what later became known as the Roosevelt Corollary to the Monroe Doctrine. A corollary states that if one thing is true, then another thing logically follows it. In this case, the Monroe Doctrine, issued in 1823, warned European countries that they must stay out of the Western Hemisphere. Roosevelt added his own interpretation to that doctrine.

"All that this country desires is to see the neighboring countries stable, orderly, and prosperous," he said. But, he added, if a nation in the Western Hemisphere did not pay its debts and failed to keep order within its borders, then the United States would exercise the use of its "international police power." In other words, the United States, not European nations, was in charge of keeping order in the Western Hemisphere.

The Dominican Republic was an example of a country that had been torn by revolutions and unrest. Rather than risk a European invasion in the Caribbean, Roosevelt arranged for the U.S. government to take over the customs offices of the Dominican Republic. Half the money received would go to pay off the country's foreign debts. The other half would go to the Dominican government to help build better schools and roads and improve health conditions.

Roosevelt was eager for the Dominicans to stand on their own without U.S. help. He knew the dangers of leaving U.S. troops abroad too long. As president he was reminded daily of the messy situation in the Philippines, where American troops were still stationed. He had inherited the war in the Philippines from McKinley, who had sent Admiral Dewey and his fleet of U.S. warships to aid the

Filipinos in their revolt against Spanish rule in 1898. The revolt had been successful, but now the new republic was having trouble establishing a stable government. Meanwhile, U.S. troops stayed on.

American military officers abroad did not always act according to Roosevelt's code of conduct. In the spring of 1903 word came down through the ranks that a U.S. officer in the Philippines was responsible for the terrible torture of prisoners of war. Burn the countryside, he had told his men. Kill children as young as ten, he had ordered. Roosevelt was angry and appalled. In a day, the officer was gone, dishonorably discharged from the army.

Nevertheless, Roosevelt continued to defend the United States' presence in the Philippines. But he was anxious to bring the U.S. troops back home; he had no intention of turning America into an empire like Great Britain, with colonies and protectorates scattered across the globe. No, he wanted the Dominicans and the Filipinos to rule themselves. Above all, he wanted to keep European and Asian powers out of the Western Hemisphere.

While Roosevelt pondered international affairs, his critics lambasted his expansionist ideas. Many Americans believed that the United States could exist without becoming involved in global affairs. Roosevelt, though, saw things differently. Countries were more interrelated now, he observed. American farmers sold grain to foreign countries, and U.S. steel was shipped abroad. Cuban sugar was found in American kitchens, and women in New York wore dresses made from imported Chinese silk. Clattering telegraph machines brought instant news from abroad to American shores. And, of course, there were countries with strong navies, countries like Japan and Germany, that tried to meddle in affairs close to America. The United States must not isolate itself from the world, Roosevelt believed. To do that would make it a second-rate country.

Roosevelt wanted the United States to be a major player on the international scene. For that to happen the country needed a canal connecting the Atlantic and Pacific Oceans. Roosevelt set out to accomplish his goal.

Chapter 16

"IN THE INTEREST OF THE UNITED STATES"

Theodore Roosevelt desperately wanted a canal. He knew that the U.S. Navy would be strengthened if it had a shorter route between the Atlantic and Pacific Oceans. During the Spanish-American War the U.S. battleship *Oregon* was lying at anchor off the California coast when the captain received orders to set sail for Cuba. The voyage, which included steaming around Cape Horn at the southern tip of Latin America, took two months. Roosevelt wanted a shorter route that would provide the U.S. Navy with more flexibility. The United States would build and operate the canal, making it open to all countries.

Everyone seemed to want the canal. The U.S. Navy wanted it. Merchants from the United States and other countries wanted it to shorten the time needed to get their goods to faraway markets. Members of the U.S. Congress wanted it. And Nicaragua wanted it. A special U.S. commission had studied possible sites for the canal and had recommended that country. The Nicaraguan government knew the building and maintenance of the canal would bring jobs and money to their country.

Not everyone wanted the canal built in Nicaragua, though. Years before, a group of French investors had formed a company to dig a canal across Panama. But after years of struggling with tropical heat, malaria, mountain terrain, and dense jungles— and financial scandals—the company had abandoned the project, leaving the equipment behind. Now Philippe Bunau-Varilla, a French engineer, wanted the United States to buy France's canal property and construction equipment. He began

Hundreds of men, laboring in tropical jungle heat to dig the Panama Canal, died of yellow fever before doctors discovered that the disease was spread by mosquitoes

lobbying to have a U.S.-controlled canal built in Panama. It would be a much better route, he said.

At first President Roosevelt was not convinced. From the maps and plans presented to him it looked as if Nicaragua had the advantage of being at sea level. Yes, Bunau-Varilla responded, but it was a longer route. If a canal with locks and dams were built in Panama, ships could pass through it in twelve hours. The Nicaraguan route would take thirty-three. Panama had the added benefit of already having construction equipment and a rail line in place. Furthermore, engineers could learn from the mistakes made by the French.

The route through Panama would not be an easy one. There were mountains to be moved, jungles to be cut through, and locks and dams to be built. But the French were willing to sell their old equipment and their rights to land across Panama to the United States. The price was forty million dollars, considerably less than the price the Nicaraguan government was suggesting. Roosevelt and Congress thought it sounded like a good deal, and in June 1902 the U.S. Senate approved the Panama route.

There was a problem, though. Panama was not an independent country. It was part of Colombia, a thin strip of land extending north from the rest of the country. And the Colombian government, headed by a corrupt dictator, was difficult to deal with. When it looked as if the U.S. favored the Nicaragua route, Colombia did everything to appear cooperative. But once Roosevelt and Congress decided on Panama, the Colombians began to balk.

When Colombia's president presented the proposed treaty with the U.S. to his government, it was rejected. Suddenly, the price they had agreed to earlier was too low. If the United States wanted to build the canal in Panama, it would have to pay more than forty million dollars. The land was so precious, the Colombians said, they would never part with it—at least not for that price.

Roosevelt was livid. The Colombians were "a lot of jack rabbits." They were "foolish and homicidal corruptionists. . . . I am not inclined to have any further dealings whatever with those . . . people," he declared.

He was determined, though, to build the canal. And he would build it in Panama. What did he need to do to make that happen, he asked Bunau-Varilla. The people of Panama wanted their independence from Colombia, the engineer replied. Perhaps the U.S. could support a revolution there.

In November 1903 the Panamanians declared themselves a separate country, independent from Colombia. Roosevelt sent a battalion of U.S. Marines to the area, and the threat of war was clear. If the Colombian government used force to put down the Panamanian rebellion, the United States would use force against Colombia. "Any interference I undertake now will be in the interest of the United States and of the people of the Panama Isthmus themselves," Roosevelt wrote to his son Kermit on November 4, 1903.

TR was determined to build a U.S. canal connecting the Atlantic and Pacific Oceans. This cartoon shows him throwing dirt on an uncooperative Colombia and supporting the Panamanian revolution.

Two days after U.S. ships arrived off its coast, Panama had a new government. And almost immediately the country signed a treaty with the United States, granting it access to the ten-mile-wide strip across its land. Now Roosevelt could build his canal.

Roosevelt had been president only three years, but in that short time he had shown the world that the United States planned on being a major global power. Nations everywhere were watching America's president.

Chapter 17

"IF ELECTED . . ."

Theodore Roosevelt had become president by a fluke. Now it was time to prove he could be elected on his own. In 1903, a year before the presidential election, he traveled across America to go camping with John Muir, a famous California naturalist. At stops all along the way, throngs of people turned out to see their new president.

He visited with old ranch friends in Medora and reminisced with them about the times they had spent together on the range. In Butte, Montana, he dined with a group of free-wheeling ranchers and businessmen who brought their guns to the table and drank heavily. He was protected by a phalanx of local sharpshooters who had been hired because of threats against him made by an anarchist labor group. Roosevelt, who had toted a loaded gun of his own since the McKinley assassination, was in his element. He had proved his physical toughness as a rancher in the Dakota Badlands and felt at home here among the rough-hewn men of the West.

The highlight of the trip, though, was the time he spent with John Muir. Together the two men took their mules, tents, bedding, and food into the quiet forests of Yosemite National Park for three days of camping and observing nature. "The first night was clear," Roosevelt wrote in his autobiography, "and we lay down in the darkening aisles of the great Sequoia grove. The majestic trunks, beautiful in color and in symmetry, rose round us like the pillars of a mightier cathedral than

Hiking in Yosemite with California naturalist John Muir was a highlight of Roosevelt's 1903 trip west.

During his 1903 trip President Roosevelt, dressed in formal clothes, shares breakfast cooked over a campfire by Colorado cowboys.

ever was conceived even by the fervor of the Middle Ages. Hermit thrushes sang beautifully in the evening, and again with a burst of wonderful music at dawn."

Roosevelt would happily have taken to the road again when the 1904 presidential campaign rolled around. But presidents didn't campaign like other candidates, he was advised. It was considered undignified and, since McKinley's assassination, perhaps unsafe. "I wish I were where I could fight more offensively," he told his friend Henry Cabot Lodge. Instead, he sat out the campaign in Washington.

He had a solid record to run on. He had taken on the most powerful financier in America and made him play by the rules. He had stepped in to negotiate a settlement to the coal strike, bringing the two sides to agreement. And the economy had remained strong in spite of the strike and his assault on the trusts.

He had given the federal government a major role to play in preserving the country's natural resources when he pushed for new conservation laws during his first years in office. He pressed Congress to pass the Reclamation Act (also known as the Newlands Act), a law that diverted water from streams and rivers into arid western lands. Money for the twenty-one irrigation projects was raised through the sale of western lands owned by the government.

On the international front he could point to the Roosevelt Corollary, his actions in the Caribbean, and the canal treaty with Panama. It was an impressive record. What's more, he was enormously popular with the voters of America.

Still, Roosevelt was nervous about the election. Mark Hanna and the wealthy Wall Street Republicans might not want to see him in the White House for another four years. He might not even get the party's nomination. He had never been

Citizens in Los Angeles turned out en masse to greet Roosevelt in 1903.

Hanna's favorite politician, and Hanna himself might want to run. But the Ohio senator knew Roosevelt would be a hard man to beat.

At the time of the Republican convention, Roosevelt had a chance to show the nation once again just how tough he could be during an international crisis. When the sultan of Morocco refused to release a U.S. citizen who had been taken captive in his country, Roosevelt sent U.S. naval ships to the area. Then he had the State Department send a telegram. "We want either Perdicaris alive or Raisuli dead," it said, referring to the captured American and the terrorist who had kidnapped him. When the delegates at the Republican convention heard those stirring words read aloud, they cheered wildly and nominated Roosevelt as their candidate. That Roosevelt—he was a fighter! He would never back down in a crisis. It looked as if Alton B. Parker, the Democrat's conservative candidate, wouldn't have a chance.

Four days before the election, Roosevelt wrote to his friend Rudyard Kipling, "If elected, I shall be very glad. If beaten I shall be sorry; but in any event I have had a first-class run for my money."

On the night of November 8, 1904, a few close friends joined Edith and Theodore in the family quarters of the White House. Archie, decorated from head to toe with campaign buttons, ran back and forth delivering the latest returns that came clicking over the telegraph machine in the West Wing. It was looking like a heady night for his father. In fact, it turned out to be a landslide. When all the votes were tallied, Theodore Roosevelt had overwhelmingly won the election for president of the United States. "I am no longer a political accident," he wrote to one of his sons.

On an overcast March day in 1905, thousands of spectators strained forward against the police barricades along Pennsylvania Avenue. They wanted to see the president as he made his way from the White House to the Capitol for his inauguration. His carriage was surrounded by members of the old Rough Rider regiment that he had led in the Spanish-American War. Bands played and banners waved in the brisk wind. Roosevelt, splendid in his silk top hat and tails, rode alone in a horse-drawn carriage. Next came the first lady in a regal dark blue outfit. With her were "Princess Alice," dressed in white, and her bespectacled brother Ted. The youngest

The sun broke through what had been a cloudy sky just moments before Theodore Roosevelt took the oath of office and delivered his inaugural address on the steps of the U.S. Capitol, March 4, 1905.

Roosevelts—Ethel, Kermit, Archie, and Quentin—rode in a third carriage with a nursemaid, who tried to make them behave in front of the cheering crowds.

As Roosevelt reached the east front of the Capitol, the sun split through the dull gray sky. Roosevelt stepped forward. Behind him stood his family; his new vice president, Charles W. Fairbanks; cabinet members; and the chief justice of the Supreme Court. Then, in the solemn tradition begun by President George Washington, Theodore Roosevelt placed his left hand on the Bible, raised his right hand, and took the presidential oath of office. Theodore Roosevelt was now president of the United States, elected in his own right and ready to take on the world.

Chapter 18

"A SQUARE DEAL"

Roosevelt had been jubilant on election night in November 1904. And he had told the press something that he would later regret.

"Under no circumstances," he had informed reporters and the nation, "will I be a candidate for or accept another nomination." He had been in office for three and half years and considered that his first term, he explained. And he had just been elected to a second one. The tradition in the United States, begun by George Washington, was that presidents would serve a maximum of two terms.

Edith knew her husband had made a mistake. Theodore loved the power of the presidency. And he had a vision for the country. He would need longer than four more years to accomplish his goals.

But the Old Guard, the wealthy Wall Street Republicans who owned the country's major industries, were not sorry to hear Roosevelt's announcement. They had poured millions of dollars into Roosevelt's campaign after he convinced them that he was not a wild-eyed reformer. He even invited J. P. Morgan to dine with him at the White House. He assured the corporate moguls that if he was elected, he would leave big business alone.

Within weeks of his inauguration, however, Roosevelt began the most dramatic reform movement ever seen in America. Henry Clay Frick, a giant in the steel industry and one of the president's largest contributors, growled, "We bought the s.o.b. and then he didn't stay bought."

It looked as if Roosevelt was out to destroy American business, industrialists grumbled. They hoped that maybe he would be a lame-duck president, a leader without a following, since he would not be running for office again.

But the Old Guard was wrong. Roosevelt had no intention of sitting idle in the White House for four years. He had work to do. He wanted "a square deal" for all Americans. And a square deal meant that railroads, meat-packing companies, factories, and other industries must change the way they treated their customers and their workers.

The railroads were Roosevelt's first target. Large, wealthy rail customers paid cheap rates to move their goods to market. They cut secret deals with the railroads and demanded rebates, or kickbacks. Meanwhile, farmers and other small shippers were charged higher rates. The practice was unfair, and Roosevelt warned that it must change.

The Interstate Commerce Commission, a government agency, had some control over the nation's railroads. The ICC should set a limit on rail rates, the president declared. Congress, however, did not like his idea. Many lawmakers were influenced by money from the railroads, and for months the argument dragged on. Old Republican friends in Congress scorned Roosevelt, and he turned to former political enemies and Democrats for support.

Some members of the press were now writing articles about corruption in the railroads and other industries. Roosevelt usually would have praised them, but surprisingly he now condemned them. The journalists were "muckrakers," he charged, who only looked down into the muck, never up to more inspirational visions. They should stick with the facts and not exaggerate. He had always encouraged investigative reporters like his friends Jacob Riis and Lincoln Steffens, but now he needed the support of conservative members of Congress. He reasoned that maybe they would help with rail reform if he sided with them against the journalists. Finally, Congress passed the Hepburn Act. It gave government control over exorbitant, unfair rail rates. It was not everything Roosevelt had hoped for, but it was a start.

Next Roosevelt turned his attention to the meat-packing industry. He had read *The Jungle*, a novel by Upton Sinclair. It described in revolting detail how meat from diseased cows, pigs, and rats made its way to American dinner tables. Everyone was horrified, including Roosevelt, who began a crusade for a meat inspection act.

Government inspectors were needed to check meat-packing plants, Roosevelt believed. And there should be another law, one that would control the making of patent medicines. Advertisements said they cured almost any ailment, but they did not. Sometimes the medicines were even dangerous. Congress was not excited about passing the Meat Inspection Act and the Pure Food and Drug Act. These acts interfered with businesses' freedom to do what they pleased. But American voters wanted to be protected. The laws were passed in June 1906, as part of Roosevelt's dream of a square deal for everyone.

Ideas for reforms continued to pour from Roosevelt's office. There should be a tax on money that children inherited from wealthy parents. And, promoting a cause dear to his heart, Roosevelt insisted that the federal government should protect its greatest treasures—its lands, it rivers, its lakes, and its forests.

Upton Sinclair's novel *The Jungle* exposed unsanitary conditions in sausage-making factories like this one. As president, TR pushed Congress to pass the Pure Food and Drug Act, which regulated meat processing and other food preparation.

Working with Gifford Pinchot, head of the U.S. Forest Service, Roosevelt came up with a proposal for saving millions of acres of western lands from development. He asked Congress to approve six new national forests. Western timber men tried to block the plan. They wanted the land for logging. They lobbied members of Congress to keep the land in private hands, but Roosevelt and Pinchot were determined to put it under federal control.

Pinchot presented Roosevelt with a draft of an executive order. It would put sixteen million acres of western land under the supervision of the federal government. Scrawling his signature at the bottom of the document, President Roosevelt made the order official. The land would be there, unspoiled and undeveloped, for future generations to enjoy.

His opponents were furious. Unfair, they cried. The president was ignoring the needs of western ranchers, timber men, and builders. But Roosevelt stood firm. The country was losing its animals, its trees, its pure rivers and streams. Americans must conserve their natural resources, he lectured. "I ask that your marvelous natural resources be handed on unimpaired to your posterity," he told a group in California. "We are not building this country of ours for a day. It is to last through the ages."

Roosevelt remembered earlier years when buffalo and elk had freely roamed America's western plains and mountains. They were almost gone now, killed by hunters. Once the United States had been covered with billions of acres of great trees. Now more than half those trees had disappeared, cut to make lumber for houses or wood pulp for paper.

Over the years he had seen rich topsoil wash away from productive farmlands. The dramatic cliffs in his beloved West had crumbled to nothingness. Erosion, poor land management practices, thoughtless hunting, and too much development were all eating away at America's unique natural resources. As president, Roosevelt believed it was his duty to preserve what he could for future generations.

Early on in his presidency, Roosevelt had pushed to bring water to dry, unproductive desert lands in the West through a network of dams and irrigation projects. By 1904 sixteen reclamation projects were under way, and builders had begun work on the giant Roosevelt Dam in Colorado. Communities sprang up, and food and jobs became plentiful.

Roosevelt takes aim during a western hunting trip. Though he was an avid hunter and loved to shoot and kill animals, Roosevelt was the first president to establish federal wildlife refuges and make land conservation a priority.

The U.S. Forest Service, established in 1905, hired more foresters and trained them to manage public lands. Until Roosevelt's time, no one knew exactly how much public land there was, or where it was located. Now surveyors and mapmakers identified the government's holdings.

There were also new protections for wildlife. When Roosevelt learned that the beautiful birds of Florida's Pelican Island were being shot by poachers for their feathers, he stepped in. Was there any reason why he could not declare the island a federal bird reservation, he asked his advisers. No, they answered. "Very well," he responded, "then I so declare it."

Until Roosevelt's administration, newspapers never included stories about conservation. Now they did. Roosevelt was a spirited spokesperson for his cause. Speeches, books, articles, conferences, arm twisting in Congress, trips with naturalists—he used all of these methods to send his message to the American public.

Each year that Roosevelt was in office the list of protected lands grew longer and more impressive: eighteen national monuments, including the Grand Canyon and Muir Woods; five new national parks; four national game preserves; fifty-one federal bird reservations; 150 national forests, and twenty-four reclamation projects. He organized seven conservation conferences and commissions. During his presidency, approximately 230 million acres of land were placed under federal protection. It was a record unequaled by any other president. And it was, perhaps, his greatest legacy.

Chapter 19

"THE BRIDE AT EVERY WEDDING"

Jean Jules Jusserand, the French ambassador in Washington, was well dressed when he arrived at the White House. After all, the president had invited him to join him on a walk in Rock Creek Park. In France a walk in the park meant a civilized stroll on well-tended, paved paths. The ambassador soon learned, though, that his topcoat and silk hat weren't appropriate for an outing with Roosevelt.

Dressed in rugged outdoor clothes and thick-soled hiking boots, Roosevelt often led Jusserand and other friends on one of his famous point-to-point hikes. The group was told they could not go around any obstacle between their starting point and their destination. The rule was under, over, or through—never around. Following Roosevelt's energetic lead, they sprinted up sheer rock cliffs, slid down rough hillsides, and made their way through thick underbrush.

In his autobiography Roosevelt told of outings in the early spring that included swimming in Rock Creek or the Potomac River, "when the ice was still thick upon it. . . . If we swam the Potomac, we usually took off our clothes." He remembered one such expedition with Ambassador Jusserand. "Just as we were about to get in and swim, somebody said, 'Mr. Ambassador, Mr. Ambassador, you haven't taken off your gloves,' to which he promptly responded, 'I think I will leave them on; we might meet ladies!'"

TR wore out many companions on his vigorous hikes and horseback rides. One senator described his own experience with the president during his early years in

A group of Roosevelt's companions scale a sheer rock cliff in Washington's Rock Creek Park on one of TR's famous point-to-point hikes.

the White House this way: "The President walked with short choppy steps. I got weary in a little while, but of course I had to keep pace with the administration and trudged along until I was pretty well worn out. To add to my discomfort, our course led through Rock Creek Park, and when we came to the stream, instead of deviating and seeking a bridge, Roosevelt strode right through the water, which was well up to the tops of his shoes, with never a break in his flow of speech, and just as if this was the most natural thing in the world to do."

But the demands of his job didn't allow Roosevelt to be outside—riding, hunting, hiking, and rowing—the way he used to. Instead, he turned to whatever sport he could perform at the White House. Unfortunately, he injured himself frequently. He sprained his ankle on the tennis court outside his office in the West Wing but kept on playing till the injury got worse. He broke his arm while stick-fighting with an old army comrade. And he pulled a muscle in his thigh, then suffered from a detached retina after boxing with a military aide. The eye never healed properly, and as he grew older, he completely lost his sight in that eye.

Roosevelt tried hard, though, to keep in shape, and he insisted that others do so, too. U.S. military officers were told that they had to be able to ride one hundred miles on horseback in three days' time. They could not possibly do that, they complained. Nonsense, Roosevelt responded. He could do that in one day. And he did, riding from the White House to Warrenton, Virginia, and back, arriving home in a blinding ice storm, exhilarated by his adventure.

While he expected much from the military, Roosevelt worried about young men on the football field. During his time in office, dozens of players had died and others had suffered serious head and neck injuries while playing the game. Roosevelt loved sports, probably more than any other president. He wanted schools to continue playing football, but safely. Something needed to be done, he concluded in the fall of 1905. He called together the coaches from the three major football colleges—Harvard, Princeton, and Yale. Before the week was up the group had agreed to enforce stricter safety rules and had set up a commission that later became the National Collegiate Athletic Association.

Roosevelt also attacked the English language. The way Americans spelled words made no sense, he said. Look at the word "through"—shouldn't it be spelled "thru," just the way it sounded? The word "kissed" should be simplified to "kist," he reasoned, and "ripped" should be "ript."

Roosevelt had never been much of a speller himself and he hadn't improved over the years. He directed the U.S. Government Printing Office to use the list of words with more logical spellings that had been compiled by Columbia University. Congress balked. They would not appropriate money for such silliness, they decided. Roosevelt had gone too far. It was, one publication wrote, "2 mutch."

While Roosevelt was busy with unfair football practices and unreasonable spellings, Edith was busy at the White House planning a wedding. Alice was head over heels in love with an Ohio congressman fifteen years older than she. She had met him in Washington and was disappointed to learn that he was interested not

TR, never the best of spellers, thought words should be written the way they sounded: "thru" for "through" and "deprest" for "depressed."

in her but in one of her close friends. When that romance failed, he turned his attention to Alice. She was elated, and Edith and Theodore, amazed that anyone wanted to marry the headstrong girl, approved.

Several years earlier Secret Service agents at Sagamore Hill had carted a young vagrant off to a mental hospital when he showed up at the gate announcing he had come to marry the president's daughter. "Of course the man was crazy," Roosevelt explained to reporters. "He wanted to marry Alice." Nick Longworth was different, though. He was, after all, a wealthy, well-bred Republican.

Alice's father was fond of laughing about his daughter's strong-minded independence. But he admired her spirit and recognized her popularity with the American public and foreign diplomats. When she was twenty-one, he sent her with a congressional delegation to Japan and China. In a stopover in Hawaii, she learned to dance the hula. She met with the Japanese emperor and China's dowager empress. And, at every stop she was greeted by adoring throngs and treated like royalty. Longworth was part of the delegation and during their trip, Alice became more and more enamored of him. Their formal engagement was announced soon after they arrived back in the States.

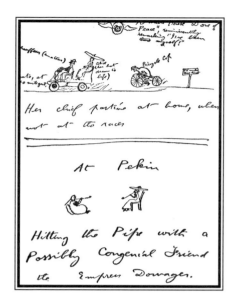

Alice was the toast of America with her good looks, high-spirited social life, and elegant clothes. Roosevelt sent her as an unofficial ambassador to China. In this letter he sketches her smoking a pipe with the dowager empress of China.

Several months later Alice stood in the doorway of the East Room in the White House in her white satin gown. Her lace veil was the one her mother, Alice Lee, had worn when she married Theodore in Chestnut Hill years before. Now Alice, the daughter who never had known her mother, took the arm of her father and proceeded down the aisle to her new husband. When it was time to give the bride away, Theodore was so overcome with emotion he could barely speak and he silently placed his daughter's hand in Longworth's.

The previous year, 1905, Roosevelt had walked another bride down the aisle. Eleanor, his shy orphaned niece who had been so overwhelmed by her rowdy Roosevelt cousins at Oyster Bay, was now a gracious, poised young woman. She had met Franklin, her handsome, ambitious fifth cousin once removed at family gatherings. He was drawn to her intelligent, kindhearted nature; they were married in Manhattan.

When the president arrived on the day of Eleanor's wedding, all eyes turned from the bridal couple to him. And as soon as the ceremony was over, guests thronged around him, following him from room to room, leaving the newlyweds

Theodore Roosevelt and Franklin Delano Roosevelt

Franklin Delano Roosevelt was a fifth cousin of Theodore Roosevelt and was often included in the raucous family gatherings at Oyster Bay. Twenty-four years younger than TR, Franklin admired his older relative, and his political career followed much the same course: assistant secretary of the navy, governor of New York, and president of the United States. There were differences, though. TR was a Republican, and FDR was a Democrat. And when Theodore ran for a third term in 1912, Franklin did not support him. But when FDR became president, he enacted some of TR's proposed reforms, such as Social Security.

abandoned and alone. "Father," Alice later observed archly, "always had to be the bride at every wedding and the corpse at every funeral."

While Alice and Eleanor were beginning their lives as young brides, two of the Roosevelt's sons were having trouble in school. Young Quentin was outgoing and bright, but he was driving his teacher crazy with his unruly behavior. He left school "without permission, and told untruths about it," Roosevelt wrote to Kermit. "I had to give him a severe whipping. Mother and I are worried about him," he confided.

Ted, the oldest son, was struggling with his classes at Harvard. The president had taken his college studies very seriously, and he expected his son to do the same. Ted, however, was not the student his father had been. Because he was the president's son, journalists and cameramen followed him everywhere on campus. It was annoying and distracting. He wanted to spend time with his friends without ending up in the newspapers the next day. He had a hard time with his work and sometimes cut classes. One day his parents received the dreaded letter from the dean: Ted was on academic probation.

The president was torn. He loved his oldest son dearly and knew the boy sometimes crumbled under too much pressure. On the other hand, Theodore and Edith expected their children to do their best. "Under no circumstances and for no reason short of sickness which makes you unable to leave your room, should you cut a lesson or a theme or fail to study hard right along," he wrote to his son. Perhaps his dorm room was too noisy to study in, Roosevelt suggested. If that was the case, he would arrange for a room off campus. On the other hand, he wrote, he did not want him to "work up to the point where you break down." And, he went on to say reassuringly, "I know you have the right stuff, and I trust you entirely."

Roosevelt himself was always able to concentrate, and he continued to read voraciously even during his years as president. On the night after his nomination to run as vice president, a day that would have exhausted most men, he sat up well into the night reading Thucydides, the Greek historian. Following a New Year's Day reception at the White House when he was president, he greeted thousands of guests, went for a ride with his family, read together with Edith, then stayed up to read more after she had gone to bed.

Roosevelt had complete powers of concentration, one senator observed, "and he could go from one subject to another, or one book to another with complete control.... He never wasted a moment. He had on his desk poetry, philosophy, fiction, works on metaphysics, psychology, zoology, and so on, and if he had ten minutes of unoccupied time, he grabbed one of these books and plunged at once into its pages."

He read tomes by Greek philosophers, long novels by Russian authors, epic poems, military histories, newspapers, magazine articles, detailed accounts of the habits of mammals, and obscure treatises on bird life. And he didn't skim. The books he read had turned-down pages and notes in the margins. He tore pages from magazine articles and left them in drifting piles on the floor around his chair.

Relaxing at a cabin in Colorado, President Roosevelt enjoys his favorite pastime as he shares a book with the dog in his lap.

Roosevelt had boundless energy, but even he needed to rest from time to time. It would be nice, Edith decided in the summer of 1905, to have a secluded retreat where she and Theodore could go, away from the distractions of the White House. The place she found was Pine Knot, a primitive log cabin nestled in the foothills of the Blue Ridge Mountains of Virginia.

"It really is a perfectly delightful little place," Theodore wrote to Kermit. "In the morning I fried bacon and eggs, while Mother boiled the kettle for tea and laid the table." Later he cut some wood and the two of them took a walk, then sat in rocking chairs and listened to the birds. At night they went to sleep with the scampering sounds of a family of flying squirrels that lived in the rafters.

It seemed almost too idyllic. One visitor asked Edith about security. Wasn't the president vulnerable to an easy attack here in this unprotected wilderness, he asked. Yes, Edith replied, she had thought of that, and she had arranged for two Secret Service men to stand guard at night. But Theodore didn't know about it. He would be annoyed.

So as Roosevelt slept peacefully in the fresh mountain air of Virginia, two armed guards stood sentinel a few hundred yards away in the dark, ready to protect their president.

Protecting the President

Much to his annoyance, Roosevelt was guarded closely by Secret Service agents once he became president. McKinley's assassination and the fear of future terrorist acts had heightened security concerns. At the White House, Oyster Bay, and Pine Knot, and when Roosevelt was on the road, agents screened his visitors and monitored his every move. Roosevelt resented their intrusion on his privacy and carried a gun of his own, which he thought was protection enough. (Members of the church he attended at Oyster Bay were upset when they saw it sticking out from his pocket.) He learned to accept the agents' presence, though, even when he went for a casual stroll on the streets of Washington.

Chapter 20

"CARRY A BIG STICK"

On a late summer afternoon in 1905 Edith Roosevelt and her children headed for the cliffs overlooking Oyster Bay. They spread out their blankets on a grassy hilltop, sat down, and looked across the water to watch an international drama unfold. There was the *Mayflower,* the presidential yacht, floating at anchor in the distance. They and hundreds of other onlookers watched as President Roosevelt boarded the yacht. Soon two cruisers steamed into the waters and sent individual launches to ferry two sets of diplomats—one Japanese and one Russian—across to the waiting president.

Russia and Japan were at war, and Roosevelt had brought the two men together to negotiate peace for their countries. It had not been easy. Russia had invaded Manchuria, violating the Open Door policy that allowed all countries equal trading access to Chinese territories. Japan, which had recently invaded China, considered Manchuria theirs. They had retaliated by attacking the Russian navy as it floated in the harbor of Port Arthur, a city in northern China. The war had been a bloody conflict, and Roosevelt feared that if it continued, the world's delicate "balance of power" would totter, allowing the stronger country to dominate the region.

The president had used every foreign contact he knew to bring the two countries together. Even Edith had been in on the plot for peace, receiving news about Russia's Czar Nicholas II through letters from a friend in St. Petersburg. Now these diplomats, representing two war-weary countries, had agreed to come together for a meeting on board a ship. First, though, they met here in Oyster Bay with President Roosevelt, the man responsible for bringing them together.

Once the diplomats were on board the *Mayflower*, Roosevelt greeted them courteously, trying to ease the distrust between the two delegations. As the diplomats climbed the gangplank to the *Mayflower*, the president stepped forward to welcome them. Both the Russian and Japanese governments were sticklers for protocol, and Roosevelt, as the representative of the United States, was careful not to favor one guest over the other. As the three headed from the deck into the galley for lunch, Roosevelt linked arms with both men and walked them across the threshold together, making sure that neither was ahead of the other.

When the diplomats traveled on to Portsmouth, New Hampshire, Roosevelt met with the ambassadors from both countries. He urged Germany's Kaiser Wilhelm II to use his influence with Czar Nicholas II. He urged the British ambassador to use his influence with the Japanese rulers.

For four weeks the talks continued, several times verging on collapse. Russia wanted land the Japanese had conquered in China. Japan insisted that Russia pay money in return. Neither party was willing to budge. At Oyster Bay, Roosevelt received reports on the negotiations. When it seemed neither country would give an inch, Roosevelt suggested alternatives. He cabled leaders in Russia and Japan, urging them to come to an agreement.

Finally, Japan broke the deadlock and accepted Russia's proposal. In early September 1905 the two countries signed the Treaty of Portsmouth, ending the war. Roosevelt's mission was accomplished. A threat to the security of the world had been eliminated. And he had been the peacemaker.

A year later, in December 1906, the president received word that he had been awarded the Nobel Peace Prize for his negotiations during the Russo-Japanese War. He was the first American ever to receive one of the cherished prizes in any field.

Peace, Roosevelt believed, naturally followed strength. "Speak softly and carry a big stick; you will go far," he said. One of the big sticks Roosevelt wanted to carry was a stronger, larger U.S. Navy. As assistant secretary of the navy, he had pushed for the building of more ships. Now, thanks in part to his planning, the U.S. fleet was the second largest in the world, outsized only by Great Britain's.

Russia and Japan had stopped fighting, but Japan was unhappy with the terms of the Treaty of Portsmouth. To make matters worse, California was discriminating against Japanese immigrants, forcing their children to attend separate schools. The Japanese government complained bitterly to Roosevelt.

America must maintain good relations with Japan, Roosevelt believed. He persuaded California and Japan to work out a compromise. If Japan would limit the numbers of immigrants coming into California, the state would drop its requirement for separate schools.

In spite of Roosevelt's efforts to maintain peace around the globe, the world

TR believed a strong navy would help push the United States into a more powerful position as a world leader. Here, he reviews the U.S. fleet from the deck of the presidential yacht *Mayflower*.

seemed in a precarious state. It was time, Roosevelt decided, to show off America's military strength. It was time to send the U.S. Navy around the world.

On a bright December day in 1907, Roosevelt stood erect on the deck of the *Mayflower* and tipped his silk top hat to the sixteen warships sailing out of Hampton Roads, Virginia. The ships were painted gleaming white rather than the usual gray. Eighteen thousand sailors on board saluted their Commander in Chief as bands played and flags snapped in the breeze. Then the ships passed into the waters of the

In 1907 Roosevelt sent the navy's Great White Fleet on a voyage around the world to show off U.S. military strength. He is shown welcoming home sailors aboard the USS *Connecticut*.

Atlantic Ocean and began their round-the-world voyage. They proceeded south toward Cape Horn, passing Central America, where thousands of Panamanians were laboring to build the canal that would shorten future voyages. At the tip of South America the vessels turned north into the Pacific. They stopped in San Francisco, then headed west for Japan. At ports of call all along their route, the sailors were greeted with an outpouring of enthusiasm for America.

Roosevelt had two things in mind when he ordered the Great White Fleet out into the world. He wanted Americans to feel pride in their country. To make sure word of the voyage got back to newspapers in the States, he arranged for a reporter to sail with the fleet.

And the president wanted other countries, especially Japan, to be impressed with America's military strength. When the ships reached Yokohama Harbor, thousands of Japanese turned out to give them a warm welcome. The fleet proceeded west and south to China and Ceylon, sailed through the Suez Canal in Egypt, crossed the Mediterranean, and set its course for home.

On February 22, 1909, fourteen months after leaving Hampton Roads, the Great White Fleet sailed triumphantly into its home port. Roosevelt and thousands of cheering Americans were there to greet it. The fleet had sailed 46,000 miles and had done what no other country's navy had ever done before: it had completely circled the globe. Ordering the voyage was, Roosevelt announced, "the most important service that I rendered to peace."

Chapter 21

"GOOD-BYE, MR. PRESIDENT"

The Panama Canal Treaty, the voyage of the Great White Fleet, reforms at home, the Nobel Prize for Peace. Roosevelt was piling up an impressive record of achievements. But not all events that happened during his presidency brought him honor.

One began in Brownsville, a Texas border town near an army base that housed the all-black 25th Regiment. On a hot August night in 1906, a riot broke out in the town, and a local man was shot and killed. White town residents claimed the black soldiers were responsible. But one white officer reported that the soldiers had been provoked by blatant discrimination on the part of the town's white citizens. Others thought perhaps the townspeople had actually started the riot themselves, then tried to pin the blame on the 25th. But when the members of the 25th closed ranks and refused to talk to officials, suspicion ran high.

Without a trial—or even an impartial investigation—the army decided that all 167 men of the regiment should be dischargd. Their silence equaled insubordination, it determined. Many of the men had been loyal members of the U.S. military for decades. Some had even served with Roosevelt in Cuba.

Roosevelt had been a champion of equal rights for all Americans for years. He valued his friendship with Booker T. Washington, the Negro educator and leader. He spoke out forcefully against lynchings in the South. He admired the all-black unit that fought next to his in the Spanish-American War. But during the Brownsville incident, Roosevelt became defensive and refused to hear any criticism of his decision. A Congressional committee examined the evidence and concluded that the men of the 25th Regiment were guilty. But no one from the regiment ever testified, and many thought the investigation was one-sided. Later some members of the 25th Regiment were allowed to reenlist. But after Brownsville many members of the black community lost their trust in Roosevelt. "The one man our race has loved best since Lincoln has betrayed us," a group of New York Negroes stated.

A year later, in 1907, another crisis threatened Roosevelt's popularity. The stock market plunged, and investors saw their savings dwindle. Wealthy Wall Street leaders growled that it was Roosevelt's fault: The president was antibusiness. As the financial crisis deepened, the U.S. government stepped in and poured money into the economy. But it wasn't enough.

The Tennessee Coal and Iron Company, one of the country's major businesses, was about to go under. J. P. Morgan met with Roosevelt and offered to buy all of the company's stock in order to keep it from failing. But he wanted to make sure that Roosevelt would not bring one of his famous antitrust cases. His offer would save the U.S. economy, Morgan promised Roosevelt.

Morgan's offer seemed reasonable, even patriotic. Could he be sure that Morgan would not profit from the buyout, Roosevelt asked the financier? Yes, Morgan responded. Then go ahead, Roosevelt told him. But once the deal was done, Roosevelt, along with the rest of America, realized that Morgan had added millions to his own personal fortune through the deal. Critics of Wall Street and big business accused Roosevelt of being soft on business and not protecting the people's interests.

Roosevelt had his critics, but he was still one of the most popular presidents the United States had ever had. The Republican Party happily would have nominated him to run again for president in the 1908 elections. American voters most certainly would have returned him to the White House. But he had vowed not to run for another term, and Roosevelt was a man of his word.

William Howard Taft, Roosevelt's friend and the current secretary of war, was the president's choice to follow him into office. He promoted him to the leaders of the Republican Party and then, after Taft won the nomination, advised him on how

Spectators risked standing on rooftops and telephone poles to catch a glimpse of their popular president.

to conduct his campaign. Smile more, he told him. Don't spend so much time playing golf and fishing—the American people want a serious candidate. Roosevelt was full of advice and high hopes for Taft. He would, Roosevelt believed, continue the policies and programs begun during his own administration.

When in November 1908 the voters chose Taft over William Jennings Bryan, Theodore Roosevelt prepared to step down. He removed the animal heads he had collected during his hunting trips from the walls of his office and packed up the hundreds of books he had brought to the White House. He made a final report to Congress and called for even more control over the railroads, more laws to protect workers, an eight-hour working day, and, of course, more protection for the nation's natural resources.

He played tennis with his "tennis cabinet," celebrated a White House Christmas with his family and friends, and threw a coming-out party for his daughter Ethel.

The evening before Taft's inauguration, snow began to fall in the nation's capital, then whirled in blizzard fury across the city. At the White House the Tafts joined the Roosevelts and some friends for dinner. Warmth glowed from the fire in

William Howard Taft, Roosevelt's friend and successor in the White House, weighed more than three hundred pounds. During the campaign TR advised him not to be photographed playing golf.

Roosevelt and Taft rode to Taft's inauguration during one of Washington's worst blizzards in decades.

the fireplace in the elegant dining room, but the dinner was a quiet, subdued affair. The Roosevelts' days in the White House had come to an end.

The next day, March 4, 1909, the snow was so heavy that the inauguration was moved from the Capitol steps to inside the U.S. Senate chambers. Theodore Roosevelt stood behind the Chief Justice of the Supreme Court and watched as William Howard Taft was sworn in as the twenty-seventh president. Then he embraced his successor and quickly left the platform. Outside, a throng of people who had gathered to bid him farewell called out, "Good-bye, Mr. President."

Roosevelt's presidency was over. For seven and a half years he had led the nation into a new era. He had maneuvered the course of the United States as it became a global leader. He had steered hostile nations toward peace in a time of war. He had navigated the choppy seas of Congress, mapped a plan for conserving the country's natural wonders, and charted a new course of fairness and square dealing for American workers. He had trimmed the sails of big business and brought the nation and its economy into a safe harbor.

And, he wrote to his son Kermit, he and Edith had "enjoyed the White House more than any other President and his wife."

Chapter 22

"MY HAT IS IN THE RING"

Books, books, books. Dozens of classics, all bound in pigskin leather and packed in wooden crates, were stacked on the pier ready to be loaded onto the *Hamburg*, a steamer docked in New York's Hudson River. Theodore Roosevelt, ex-president of the United States, was going on a trip. And TR never went far without a book.

It was a hunting trip or, as Roosevelt preferred to call it, a scientific expedition. He and his nineteen-year-old son Kermit would be gone for a year. The books were only part of the luggage. There were maps, rifles, tents, canned goods, and champagne. And there was salt, four tons of it, needed to preserve the animals they planned to shoot.

"Hooray for Africa," Roosevelt had written in a letter while he was still in Washington. Now, less than three weeks after leaving office, together with Kermit, he was about to fulfill his lifelong dream to go on a safari.

When they reached central Africa, Roosevelt was enthralled. Exotic birds flew nearby, and the hills and grasses were thick with hyenas, giraffes, and antelope. Joining him on the journey were scientists from the Smithsonian Institution, hunters, native soldiers, taxidermists, and more than two hundred porters to carry baggage.

Roosevelt was an experienced hunter. He had bagged bears, elk, and buffalo in the American West. But now he wanted to hunt the rhinos, elephants, lions, and leopards that he could find only in Africa. He shot his first lion in the early days of

After Taft's inauguration, TR left for a hunting trip in Africa. His luggage included crates of supplies and books.

the trip, and before the trip was over he and Kermit had killed more than five hundred of Africa's wild animals.

Roosevelt planned to bring home several trophies for the walls at Oyster Bay. But the real purpose of the trip was to collect hundreds of large mammals that would be mounted and put on display at the Smithsonian in Washington, D.C. For almost a year Roosevelt hunted, helped the taxidermists, camped, and visited with friends living in Africa.

And he wrote. Each night the former president retired early to his tent and poured onto paper his impressions of the land, the people, and the animals of Africa. Back home in the States, Roosevelt's fans waited eagerly for the next installment of their hero's adventures, which were published in *Scribner's* magazine.

Kermit accompanied his father to Africa, where TR shot 296 animals, including lions, elephants, rhinoceroses, hippopotamuses, zebras, and gazelles. Here, father and son sit on a slain buffalo.

"I speak of Africa and golden joys," he wrote, "the joy of wandering through lonely lands, the joy of hunting the mighty and terrible lords of the wilderness." He told in dramatic detail the killing of his first lion with the animal's "lips drawn up in a prodigious snarl." He described the "large tropic moons, and the splendor of the new stars," and the "wide waste spaces of earth, unworn of man."

Roosevelt loved his African adventure. But he was homesick. After twelve months away, he was overjoyed when Edith made the trip up the Nile and met him in Khartoum. Together the couple traveled to Egypt, Italy, France, Germany, Norway, Sweden, and England. Everywhere, they were greeted like royalty. Throngs of curious spectators turned out to see the legendary American president. In Norway he stopped to receive the Nobel Peace Prize, which he had been awarded in 1906, and said in a speech that the world should establish a League of Peace. But, he cautioned, the world must also be prepared to fight for freedom.

He met with Kaiser Wilhelm II and reviewed German troops—the same troops that within only a few years would be fighting against American soldiers. He gave lectures at esteemed European universities, received honorary degrees, and laughed when a small teddy bear was lowered from the ceiling during one of the somber ceremonies.

When Edward VII, king of England, died in May 1910, President Taft asked Roosevelt to represent the United States at the funeral. He paid tribute to England and its monarch in a ceremony that included all the European heads of state. He met with famous authors, historians, and socialites. He was the toast of Europe and Great Britain.

When TR and Edith arrived back in the United States on June 18, 1910, tens of

Former President Roosevelt is shown here visiting Napoleon's tomb in Paris.

Franklin Delano Roosevelt and his wife, Eleanor *(far right, under smokestack)*, were among the family, friends, and newsmen who gave TR a hero's welcome as he sailed home into New York Harbor in 1910.

thousands of New Yorkers crowded the docks to welcome them home. A twenty-one-gun salute boomed forth across the water, tugboats blared their horns, battleships sounded their bells, and fireboats sprayed fountains of water into the air. Throngs of citizens jammed the streets as Roosevelt and his entourage rode up Broadway, with a military band and a group of the Rough Riders leading the parade. America's hero was home, on U.S. soil, and he was more popular than ever.

In Washington, D.C., President Taft must have been slightly envious of his friend's welcome back into the country. Roosevelt had left the United States after Taft's inauguration on purpose. He did not want to look over the shoulder of the man he had handpicked to carry on his presidency. But neither Roosevelt nor the American public was very happy with Taft's performance so far.

Roosevelt had fought for the reform of child labor laws and begun a massive program to protect the country's natural resources. He had curbed big business and pushed for government regulation of factories, packing plants, and railroads. Taft, on the other hand, was not supporting Roosevelt's programs as vigorously as he had promised.

Roosevelt was disappointed in Taft, but he refused to intervene. He traveled west, spent time with his new granddaughter, read, and went for long rides. There were no more vigorous hikes or tennis matches. His body ached with rheumatism. Politics and public speaking attracted him less than before. "Home, wife, children—they are what really count in life," he wrote to his eldest son.

Not everyone wanted Roosevelt to relax into retirement, though. Throughout the country there were people unhappy with Taft's cozy relationship with big business. They needed Roosevelt's support in pushing an agenda of government reforms.

Ever the adventurer, TR took an airplane ride in St. Louis in 1910, when aviation was still new. He was the first president to fly in an airplane, go down in a submarine, own a car, and have a telephone in his home.

Finally, after months of holding back, Roosevelt began to speak out. Children and women should not have to work such long hours, he declared. Workers should receive compensation if they were injured on the job. They should have the right to organize and to bargain for their rights with their employers.

Roosevelt's supporters in the business world were appalled by his proposals. And President Taft, who had counted on his old friend to support him during his bid for reelection, began to worry about Roosevelt's loyalty. The former president was, after all, still tremendously popular and might well be elected if he chose to challenge Taft.

When the time came for Republicans to choose their nominee for the 1912 election, many delegates wanted Roosevelt, not Taft. And Roosevelt was ready to run. Yes, he told a reporter, he remembered saying back in 1904 that he would not run again for president. But things were different now. "Frequently when asked to take another cup of coffee at breakfast, I say, 'No thank you, I won't take another cup.' This does not mean that I intend to never take another cup of coffee during my life," he explained rather lamely.

In January 1912 Roosevelt told a friend, "If the people make a draft on me, I shall not decline to serve." By February he was more decisive. "My hat," he said, "is in the ring." Taft was devastated. His closest friend and political adviser had turned against him.

Old friends and loyal Republicans were torn. They had supported Roosevelt when he was president. But Taft was the president now, and they felt they must work for his reelection, not Roosevelt's.

But Roosevelt charged into the campaign with high-voltage enthusiasm. He traveled west again, this time stopping for campaign speeches along the way. He lambasted the current president. Taft has no more brains than a guinea pig, he said. He would give the voters a "square deal," the old Rough Rider promised. And his listeners believed him. In the eleven states that held primaries, voters chose Roosevelt over Taft, even in Taft's home state of Ohio.

But the presidential nominee was not chosen by the popular vote. The nominee was chosen by party delegates at the national convention. When Republican delegates gathered in Chicago for the convention, Roosevelt and his supporters faced

Unhappy with President Taft's policies, TR threw his "hat in the ring" and ran in a three-way race for president on the Progressive, or "Bull Moose," ticket in 1912.

powerful committees controlled by Taft supporters. Taft's men would control who became a delegate, not Roosevelt.

It was a "great crime," Roosevelt thundered. The people of America were behind him. The nomination should go to the man with the popular vote, not the man supported by corrupt party officials. "We stand at Armageddon, and we battle for the Lord," he proclaimed.

In the end, though, the party regulars won out. Taft was chosen as the Republican Party's nominee for president. The Democrats chose Woodrow Wilson, the governor of New Jersey and, according to Roosevelt, "pretty thin material for a president."

Enraged and bitter at being denied the nomination by his old party, Roosevelt vowed to run anyway. He would form a third party, the Progressive Party. When a reporter asked Roosevelt how he felt, he replied, "I feel as strong as a bull moose," and the Progressives became known as the Bull Moose Party. He would take with him like-minded supporters. We shall, Roosevelt announced, "fight to the end, win or lose."

Chapter 23

"THE RIGHTS OF THE PEOPLE"

October 1912, just three weeks to go before the election. Roosevelt's campaign train was snaking into Milwaukee. His speech, written on a bulky sheaf of papers, was folded into the breast pocket of his coat. His eyeglasses were there, too, in a metal case. Since childhood Roosevelt had relied on his glasses to help his acute nearsightedness. Now, armed with his speech, his glasses, and his passion, he was ready to carry his message of progressive reform to the voters of Wisconsin.

Then, as he headed from the hotel to the auditorium where he was to make his speech, a bullet thudded against Roosevelt's chest. He had been shot at close range by a crazed assassin, who later claimed he had been urged on by the ghost of William McKinley. Roosevelt slumped over in the carriage, blood pouring from his wound. The folded speech and the metal eyeglass case had kept the bullet from searing directly into his heart. They had, in fact, saved his life. But the bullet had entered his body and now lay lodged in his chest muscles. He must go to the hospital at once, doctors insisted. No, Roosevelt argued. He was not mortally wounded. He would go ahead and make his speech.

Before the horrified audience, Roosevelt stood at the podium in his blood-stained shirt and told his listeners "I have just been shot; but it takes more than that to kill a Bull Moose." Then, ignoring the pain and blood from his wound, he went on to deliver what seemed like a farewell speech. "No man," he told the group, "has had a happier life than I have led." The color drained from his face.

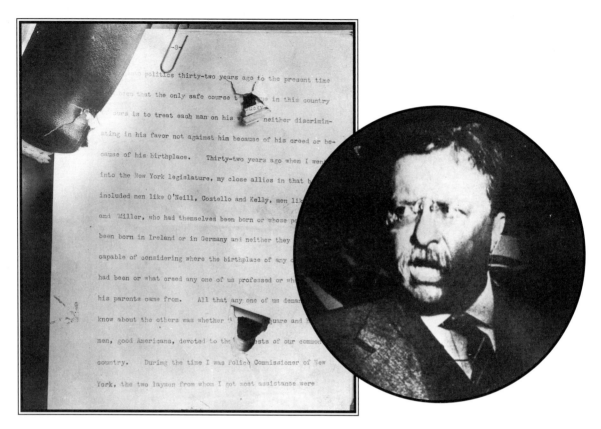

Roosevelt's metal eyeglass case *(upper left)* and thick speech *(shown pictured with bullet holes)* helped save the presidential candidate's life. Bleeding, with the bullet still in his body, he insisted on speaking for an hour and a half before a stunned audience.

Still he continued to speak for an hour and a half before he allowed doctors to rush him to the hospital. Within two weeks he was back on the campaign trail.

Just as he had predicted, Roosevelt was as strong as a Bull Moose during his campaign. Throughout the country he cajoled crowds to vote the Progressive ticket. The federal government must regulate businesses. It should raise taxes on corporations. Young children shouldn't work in mines and factories, and women shouldn't work such long hours. The Progressive Party would pass a child labor law, he promised. And there should be an eight-hour day for all workers.

Workers should have the right to organize and belong to unions, he argued. And they should be able to negotiate with their employers for better wages and working

Theodore Roosevelt's View of Women

Roosevelt believed that women were as bright and capable as men. In his senior thesis at Harvard, "Practicability of Giving Men and Women Equal Rights," he proposed that marriage laws should provide the same privileges for both sexes. Women should be allowed to keep their maiden names and be able to vote if they wanted to. Basically, though, Roosevelt believed a woman's primary duty to her country was to raise a good family— ideally, a large one. To his mind, families were more important than voting, and men should help out with child rearing. "I have mighty little use for the man who is always declaiming in favor of an eight-hour day for himself who does not think anything at all of having a sixteen-hour day for his wife." A man's duty, on the other hand, was to defend his country if necessary. When TR led the Progressive Party, he heartily endorsed the platform calling for a national law that would allow women to vote.

conditions. "If I were a wage worker, I should certainly join a union," he told one audience.

Women should have the vote, Roosevelt stated. He had had that belief from the time he was at Harvard, and he had even written a paper pointing out why women should have equal rights with men. Now he had a chance to deliver the message to the entire nation. The Progressive Party was the only major party to welcome women delegates at their convention, he told them proudly.

All over the country, speaking from the back of trains and in crowded hotel dining rooms, Roosevelt promoted the Progressive platform. Workers should be paid a minimum wage, set by the government. Factories and mines should be examined by government inspectors for safe working conditions. Farmers should receive help

On May 6, 1912, these women paraded in New York City in favor of voting rights for women, a move supported by the Progressive Party's platform.

from their government. The government should provide insurance for sick or retired workers.

Then there was Roosevelt's most controversial idea: he would reform the court system. If the public did not like a judge's ruling in a particular case, voters should be allowed to challenge the verdict. "We stand for the rights of the people," he wrote to fellow Progressives. "We are committed to the doctrine of using the National power to any extent that the rights of people demand."

Many of Roosevelt's wealthy and powerful friends from New York and Washington abandoned him. He had gone crazy, they murmured. They shunned him at parties and at gatherings where he had once been the most honored guest. Henry Cabot Lodge, one of his oldest and dearest friends, denounced him. Still Roosevelt doggedly crisscrossed the country in his effort to regain the White House.

Eleanor, his niece, remained loyal, but she could not persuade her husband, Franklin Delano Roosevelt, to join the ranks of TR supporters. It was lonely, TR confessed to a friend, to be rejected by his own kind. His ideas seemed radical in 1912. Two decades later, though, when Franklin became president, he pushed through many of the same reforms Cousin Ted had so daringly proposed.

But the country was not ready for such reform when Theodore Roosevelt sought a new term as president. The three-way race between Roosevelt, Taft, and Wilson, was decided on November 5, 1912. Roosevelt received more votes than Taft, but both the Republicans and the Progressives were defeated. Woodrow Wilson was elected president of the United States.

Roosevelt put up a good front. "We have fought the good fight, we have kept the faith, and we have nothing to regret," he wrote to a friend. But Edith and some of his closest friends knew how much the loss had hurt. And after months of vigorous campaigning, what would he do next? He had never been one to sit still for long. It was no surprise, then, when he came up with an idea for a new project.

He would become an explorer.

Chapter 24

"MY LAST CHANCE TO BE A BOY"

We are now in a hot little sidewheel steamer jammed with men, dogs, bags and belongings, partially cured and rather bad-smelling skins, and the like," Theodore wrote to Edith on Christmas Eve 1913. "I am drenched with sweat most of the waking hours, and the nights are too hot for really comfortable sleeping as a rule.... In ten days we shall be at the last post office...and then we shall go into the real wilderness."

Roosevelt was in Brazil, preparing for a perilous trip down the River of Doubt, uncharted waters that flowed through a dense and unfriendly jungle. The trip was, he told friends, his "last chance to be a boy."

Together with his son Kermit, several Brazilians, and a team of naturalists from the American Museum of Natural History, the group hacked their way through the jungle with machetes, waded through marshes, and paddled dugout canoes into the hostile, tropical territory. No explorers had ventured there before.

The rapids on the river were vicious and swept away a number of the group's canoes. One guide drowned. Another went mad, murdered one of the party, and disappeared into the jungle. Roosevelt and the rest of the party were beset by mosquitoes, wasps, vampire bats, piranhas, and flesh-eating ants. They fell ill with jungle fever and ran low on food.

The most dangerous disaster occurred when Roosevelt plunged into the fast-flowing river to rescue a marooned canoe. Struggling against the relentless current,

After losing the election, TR and his son Kermit went on an expedition down the uncharted River of Doubt in Brazil. Here the group stops for a meal in the dense jungle.

he was pinned down and smashed his leg against a rock. He had wounded the same leg in 1902 in a carriage accident, and it had never healed properly. Now it became infected. Unable to walk, he developed a high fever and had to be carried. Other men in the party were sick, too. Go ahead without him, he pleaded with Kermit. But together the group continued its tortuous way through the jungle.

After two grueling months, they reached civilization. "We have had a hard and somewhat dangerous but very successful trip," Roosevelt wrote. "We have put on the map a river about 1500 kilometers in length. . . . Until now its upper course has been utterly unknown to everyone, and its lower course . . . utterly unknown to all cartographers." In honor of their expedition, the Brazilian government renamed the river, christening it the Rio Roosevelt. Some called it the Rio Teodoro.

During his Brazilian adventure, Roosevelt lost fifty-seven pounds and much of the boyish spirit that had propelled him all his life. Now he walked with a cane and looked older and more frail. Oyster Bay and the United States seemed a safe haven after his dangerous South American adventure. But there were greater dangers lurking on the horizon, Roosevelt discovered on his return home. Europe was about to go to war. It would have been a good time for him to be in the White House, Roosevelt thought. Instead, he settled into a quiet life at Oyster Bay. "I never wish to leave Sagamore again," he wrote to his daughter.

But peace was not in the picture for Roosevelt or for the world. When Kaiser Wilhelm II of Germany ordered his troops to invade Belgium, the former president watched anxiously as the balance of power unraveled. Soon Austria-Hungary and Turkey had joined with Germany in its fight against the Allied forces of France, England, Serbia, Russia, and Italy.

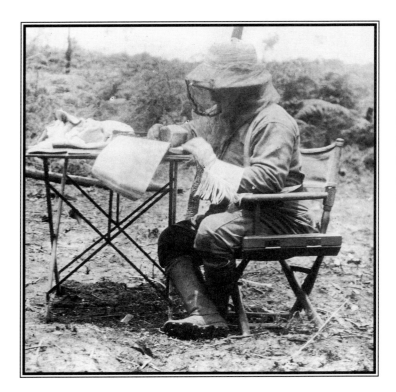

Beset by mosquitoes and suffering from the effects of insufficient food, heavy rains, killer river currents, and jungle fever, Roosevelt still made time to write articles for *Scribner's* magazine about his Brazilian adventure.

The furnishings at Sagamore Hill included some of TR's most beloved treasures: books, stuffed animal heads and skins collected during his hunting trips, a painting of his father, a desk for writing, and a portrait of President Lincoln. Jacob Riis remembered tripping over a bearskin rug each time he visited.

The United States will remain neutral, President Wilson announced. Wilson should have protested Germany's invasion of Belgium, Roosevelt told his friends. He should be building the country's military force. The United States must negotiate from a position of strength.

On May 7, 1915, a tremendous explosion tore through the hull of the *Lusitania*, a British luxury liner sailing off the coast of Ireland. When the death toll was final, more than one thousand passengers and crew members had lost their lives to a torpedo launched by a nearby German submarine. The ship, the Germans alleged, had been carrying arms for Allied forces. Among the dead passengers were 128 U.S. citizens.

Americans were stunned. Germany must apologize and pay reparations, Wilson declared sternly. And they must refrain from attacking any more passenger ships. Roosevelt was outraged at Wilson's response. "Every soft creature, every coward and weakling, every man who can't look more than six inches ahead, every man whose god is money, or pleasure, or ease...is enthusiastically in favor of Wilson," he said. Angrily he spoke out against the "peace people," Wilson, and German-Americans who put loyalty to their old homeland above their loyalty to the United States.

Roosevelt had always been proud of America's melting pot and had supported better working conditions for immigrant workers. But now he railed against "hyphenated" Americans—citizens who referred to themselves as Irish-Americans and German-Americans and so on. There was only one thing to be, he proclaimed, and that was an *American*. He admired decent, hard-working Americans of German descent, but "the professional hyphenated German-Americans I shall smite with the sword of the Lord."

Roosevelt's strong language offended many of his listeners. Others, though, heard his old passion and vigor. Perhaps he would run for president in 1916, they speculated. Buoyed by his commitment to war, Roosevelt took his message to the people. If they wanted a president who would lead them into battle, he was their man.

In June 1916 Republican delegates again traveled to Chicago to pick a presidential candidate. At Oyster Bay, perhaps Theodore Roosevelt hoped he would receive a call that would tell him he was the party's choice. Hundreds of delegates had cheered for more than half an hour when his name was placed in nomination. But the phone call never came. The Republicans chose Charles Evans Hughes, a conservative Supreme Court judge, as their presidential candidate.

Across town in Chicago the Progressives were holding their convention. Unlike the Republicans, they were delighted to nominate Theodore Roosevelt, and when the announcement was made, the crowd went wild. A few minutes later, though, the mood in the hall changed. A telegram had just arrived from Oyster Bay. Roosevelt was honored to be nominated, it said, but he would not run. Roosevelt knew from experience that third-party candidates never won elections. And if he could not lead the Republicans, he did not have the heart for a losing campaign.

Devastated, Progressive delegates tore their Roosevelt badges from their jackets and threw them to the floor. Their hero had deserted them. The Progressive Party was dead. And in November 1916 Woodrow Wilson was reelected to a second term.

The presidential campaign was over. But Roosevelt had one more campaign to wage. He wanted to be a soldier again if and when the country went to war. And for that he would have to have President Wilson's approval.

The war wasn't long in coming. After Germany torpedoed three American ships, Wilson finally gave up all hope of negotiating peace. On April 6, 1917, the United States declared war on Germany.

Eight days later Theodore Roosevelt sat in the Oval Office of the White House. It was hard to ask a favor of the man for whom he had so little respect. But he did. Would President Wilson give him permission to raise a volunteer division to fight in France?

Wilson had met Roosevelt twice before. They had run against each other in the election of 1912, and Roosevelt had said terrible things about him. But during this visit Wilson was charmed. "He is a great big boy. . . . You can't resist the man. I can see why his followers are so fond of him," he said after the meeting. But he did resist Roosevelt's request. There would be no Roosevelt volunteer division. It would interfere with supplying and training the regular troops, Wilson told him. Roosevelt never forgave him.

He would have to sit out the war at Oyster Bay. His sons, however, would not. Kermit, not willing to wait for the United States to declare war, joined the British army, later signing on with the American forces. Quentin, whose eyesight was less than perfect, memorized the letters and numbers on the eye chart in order to pass the examination to become a pilot in the Army Air Corps. Ted and Archie joined the U.S. Army. Their sister Ethel became a nurse in a hospital in France, where her husband was serving as a surgeon. Edith and Theodore were left behind at Sagamore Hill, now sadly silent.

There were grandchildren, of course, to keep the Roosevelts distracted from their constant worry about their sons. And Theodore kept up a busy schedule. He wrote a weekly news column for the *Outlook,* a national magazine, published articles in the *Kansas City Star,* and made speeches urging Americans to buy war bonds.

A loving grandfather holds Kermit Roosevelt Jr.

He criticized Wilson for the way he was conducting the war and called for support for the Red Cross. Roosevelt was more popular than ever and many Republicans' first choice for president in 1920.

He was almost sixty now, but his old passion for progressive causes still burned bright. Businesses should not profit from the war, he declared. Wealthy young men who could afford to go to college should not be excused from fighting abroad—they should serve, just like poor and uneducated Americans. Older Americans should receive pensions, and workers should receive unemployment insurance. Roosevelt was developing a platform that he thought would defeat Wilson if he ran against him in two years.

And he healed old political wounds. In Chicago, Roosevelt was eating dinner at a Chicago hotel and glanced up to see William Howard Taft, his former friend-turned-enemy. The two had recently exchanged letters, sharing their dissatisfaction with Wilson. When he saw Taft, Roosevelt got to his feet and extended his hand. Others in the dining room looked on with approval and applauded as the two former presidents sat down and spent half an hour in friendly conversation.

Roosevelt kept busy, but he worried constantly about his sons. Ted, the oldest, who had been wounded and gassed, was awarded the Distinguished Service Cross and Silver Star. Archie almost lost his leg and received the French Croix de Guerre. Their father was torn between pride and anxiety.

Then there was Quentin, the youngest. It had been a wrench for his parents to see him go. He seemed so young, and he had just gotten engaged to be married. "Q," they had called him when he was a boy. He had led his gang of friends into countless escapades back in the White House years. Edith and Theodore had wrung their hands when they learned he skipped school. Later, though, he had come to share his father's love of reading, never going far without a book. Now he was going to war.

From the front he wrote letters home about the excitement of flying, of his first dogfight with the Germans, of downing his first German plane. Then there was another flight, one in which he was separated from the others in his squadron and surrounded by seven German planes.

It was a reporter who brought the word to Roosevelt at Oyster Bay. His newspaper had received a telegram. The message was vague and incomplete: "Watch Sagamore Hill for ———." Nothing more. But when the reporter shared its contents with Roosevelt, the former president sensed what the complete message would say. The next morning a more detailed telegram was delivered to Sagamore Hill. Quentin had been shot down behind enemy lines. Three days later the Germans confirmed Quentin's death. He was buried near where his plane went down, with full military honors.

"Our pride," Roosevelt bravely told reporters, "equals our sorrow." It was hardest for Edith, he wrote to a friend. "Her heart will ache for Quentin until she dies." But it was hard for him, too. The boy in Roosevelt died when he learned of Quentin's death, a friend observed.

It was not easy to go on, but it had never been in Roosevelt's nature to quit. Republicans in New York wanted him to run for governor of their state, but he was saving himself. "I have but one good fight left in me," he told his sister Bamie. That fight was to be for his return to the White House in 1920.

In spite of his failing health and the sorrow in his heart, he continued his attacks on Wilson and the Democrats. Wilson had come up with Fourteen Points that he

An aging Roosevelt waves his hat to a crowd of admirers in 1918, the year before his death.

planned to use to end the war. They were nothing more than "fourteen scraps of paper," Roosevelt scoffed. He campaigned for Republican candidates during the midterm elections in 1918; they won. The country was ready to support him for his return to the White House, he felt.

But Roosevelt's body was giving out. His old leg wound from Brazil still plagued him. He spent a month in the hospital and came home deaf in one ear. He had trouble keeping his balance, and he had completely lost his sight in one eye. His joints continued to ache with painful rheumatism.

He returned to the hospital, plagued with a combination of ailments. From his hospital bed he met with visitors, wrote letters, composed his weekly political column for the *Kansas City Star,* and kept up his attack on Wilson. And he and Republican leaders planned his return to the White House. But it was not to be.

He was home for Christmas Day. At Oyster Bay he was surrounded by his books, his family, their children, and his beloved Edith. But he mainly stayed upstairs now, sitting in a chair in a bedroom near the window overlooking the water.

On the night of January 5, 1919, he sat with Edith. He was reading, of course. Looking up from his book he said, "I wonder if you will ever know how I love Sagamore Hill." Later the light was turned out, and he slept. He never woke.

Roosevelt had always said he wanted to "wear out, not rust out." He had followed his own advice, seizing every opportunity that came his way. Unlike many other famous presidents, he had had no major war or financial depression that pushed him to lead the country. Instead, he had created his own momentum.

"I put myself in the way of things happening," he once told Jacob Riis, "and they happened."

Source Notes

The quotations that appear as chapter titles are from the following sources:

Introduction: address to the Hamilton Club of Chicago, April 10, 1899
Chapter 1: letter to his mother, written from Harvard University, November 19, 1876
Chapter 2: letter to his wife, Alice Lee Roosevelt, written from Albany, February 6, 1884
Chapter 3: *Theodore Roosevelt: An Autobiography*, p. 94
Chapter 4: letter to Jonas Van Duzer, a former colleague in the New York State Assembly, January 15, 1888
Chapter 5: letter to Henry Cabot Lodge, June 24, 1889
Chapter 6: letter to his sister Anna, May 19, 1895
Chapter 7: letter to Bellamy Storer, August 19, 1897
Chapter 8: letter to his sister Corinne from onboard the *Yucatan* as it sailed from Tampa to Cuba, June 15, 1898
Chapter 9: letter to Henry Cabot Lodge, April 27, 1899
Chapter 10: letter to Henry Cabot Lodge, December 11, 1899
Chapter 11: *Theodore Roosevelt: An Autobiography*, p. 364
Chapter 12: *Theodore Roosevelt: An Autobiography*, p. 349
Chapter 13: letter to his son Ted, October 19, 1901
Chapter 14: letter to Mark Hanna, October 3, 1902
Chapter 15: policy stated in annual address to Congress, December 6, 1904
Chapter 16: letter to his son Kermit, November 4, 1903
Chapter 17: letter to Rudyard Kipling, November 1, 1904
Chapter 18: address delivered at the New York State Fair in Syracuse, September 3, 1903
Chapter 19: comment to a friend by Alice Roosevelt Longworth
Chapter 20: an African proverb frequently quoted by Roosevelt
Chapter 21: newspaper reports of Roosevelt's departure from Taft's inauguration ceremony, March 4, 1909, cited in Edmund Morris's *Theodore Rex*, p. 552
Chapter 22: remark to a reporter in 1912 prior to his formal announcement as a presidential candidate for the Progressive Party, cited in H. W. Brands's *T.R.: The Last Romantic*, p. 703
Chapter 23: letter to the Progressives in Congress, April 2, 1913
Chapter 24: comment to friends prior to his departure for Brazil

Bibliography

BOOKS

There are hundreds of books by and about Theodore Roosevelt, and new ones appear each year. Here are a few favorites.

To capture young Teedie's spirit through his own words, read *The Boyhood Diary of Theodore Roosevelt, 1869–1870: Early Travels of the 26th President* (Mankato, Minn.: Blue Earth Books, 2001). *A Bully Father: Theodore Roosevelt's Letters to His Children* (New York: Random House, 1995) offers delightful glimpses of Roosevelt's dedication to his family. H. W. Brands's *The Selected Letters of Theodore Roosevelt* (New York: Cooper Square, 2001) provides a manageable, one-volume collection of his correspondence, revealing Roosevelt's energy, humor, and broad range of interests. For a more complete view of Roosevelt's correspondence, Elting Morison's eight-volume compilation, *The Letters of Theodore Roosevelt* (Cambridge, Mass.: Harvard University Press, 1951–54), spans his lifetime and his connections with a vast array of friends, relatives, conservationists, authors, military strategists, and world leaders. The collection is now out of print, but it is available in many libraries.

To better understand Roosevelt's attachment to the American West, read his letter to Secretary of State John Hay (August 9, 1903), which describes his encounters during his two-month trip across the country. Roosevelt also reveals his deep connection with the West in his *Hunting Trips of a Ranchman* and *The Wilderness Hunter* (New York: Modern Library, 1996). His experiences as a big-game hunter and explorer are colorfully described in his *African Game Tales* (New York: St. Martin's, 1988) and *Through the Brazilian Wilderness* (Birmingham, Ala.: Palladium, 2000).

Reminiscences by family members can be found in *My Brother, Theodore Roosevelt* (reissued in paperback, 2001) by Roosevelt's sister Corinne Roosevelt Robinson and in *Crowded Hours* (New York: Arno, 1980), an autobiography by Roosevelt's daughter Alice Roosevelt Longworth. Sylvia Jukes Morris's biography *Edith Kermit Roosevelt: Portrait of a First Lady* (New York: Modern Library, 2001) provides a look at the life of Theodore's second wife and the Roosevelt children. Jacob Riis and John Burroughs give their respective impressions of their association with TR in *Theodore Roosevelt: The Citizen* (St. Clair Shores, Mich.: Scholarly Press, 1970) and *Camping and Tramping with President Roosevelt* (New York: Arno, 1970).

Recommended biographies include David McCullough's *Mornings on Horseback* (New York: Simon & Schuster, 1981), which focuses on Roosevelt's life from his birth through his marriage to Edith Carow; Edmund Morris's *The Rise of Theodore Roosevelt* (New York: Modern Library, 2001), which chronicles his life from infancy through his vice presidency, and *Theodore Rex* (New York: Random House, 2001), covering the events of his life as president; and H. W. Brands's one-volume biography, *T.R.: The Last Romantic* (New York: Basic Books, 1997). James MacGregor Burns and Susan Dunn analyze the social and political influence of Theodore, Eleanor, and Franklin in *The Three Roosevelts: Patrician Leaders Who Transformed America* (New York: Atlantic Monthly Press, 2001).

WEBSITES

An Internet search for Theodore Roosevelt will bring up more than 200,000 entries. The best place to start is the excellent and extensive site maintained by the Theodore Roosevelt Association, www.theodoreroosevelt.org. It provides biographical profiles (including one by his oldest son, Theodore Roosevelt Jr.), photographs, texts of speeches, cartoons, and a wealth of other information. It also provides links to other reliable Roosevelt websites.

VIDEOS

TR: The Story of Theodore Roosevelt: The American Experience, PBS

Theodore Roosevelt: Rough Rider to Rushmore, A&E Biography Series

The Indomitable Teddy Roosevelt, Signal Hill Entertainment

My Father the President, tour of Sagamore Hill with audio by Roosevelt's daughter, Ethel Roosevelt Derby

Places to Visit

Theodore Roosevelt Birthplace National Historic Site
28 East 20th Street
New York, New York 10003
(212) 260-1616

Sagamore Hill National Historic Site
20 Sagamore Hill Road
Oyster Bay, New York 11771-1809
(516) 922-4447 for 24-hour recorded information

Theodore Roosevelt Inaugural National Historic Site
641 Delaware Avenue
Buffalo, New York 14202
(716) 884-0095
email: THRI_Administration@nps.gov

Theodore Roosevelt National Park
Medora, North Dakota (South Unit)
Watford City, North Dakota (North Unit)
(701) 623-4466
(701) 842-2333
email: THRO_interpretation@nps.gov

Pine Knot
Albemarle County, Virginia
Advance arrangements for visits may be made by writing:
Pine Knot
P.O. Box 213
Keene, Virginia 22946

Mount Rushmore National Memorial
Keystone, South Dakota
(605) 574-3171
Site of 60-foot-high sculptures of U.S. presidents George Washington, Thomas Jefferson,
Theodore Roosevelt, and Abraham Lincoln

Chronology of Events in the Life of Theodore Roosevelt

1858	October 27	Born in New York City, the second child of Theodore and Martha Roosevelt; siblings include Anna (Bamie or Bye), Elliott, and Corinne
1876	September	Enters Harvard University
1878	February 9	Death of his father in New York City
1880	June 30	Graduates with honors from Harvard University
	October 27	Marries Alice Hathaway Lee in Brookline, Massachusetts
1881	November 8	At age 23 is the youngest man elected to the New York State Assembly, where he serves three terms
1883	September	Travels west to the Dakota Badlands and buys a herd of cattle to run on the Maltese Cross Ranch
1884	February 12	Birth of daughter Alice Lee Roosevelt at family home in New York City
	February 14	Unexpected death of wife and mother in family home in New York City
	June	Delegate to national Republican convention
	June	Leaves for the Badlands, buying more cattle and building a house on the Elkhorn Ranch, where he lives as a rancher for two years; his infant daughter, Alice, stays in New York with Theodore's sister Anna
1886	November 2	Defeated as candidate for mayor of New York City
	December 2	Marries Edith Kermit Carow, childhood friend, in a private ceremony in London
1887		Earns living as an author (he published thirty-five books during his lifetime)
	September 13	Birth of son, Theodore Roosevelt Jr., at new home, Sagamore Hill, in Oyster Bay on New York's Long Island

1888	January	Founds Boone and Crockett Club with fellow conservationist George Bird Grinnell
1889	May 7	Appointed U.S. Civil Service commissioner in Washington, D.C., where he serves until May 1895
	October 10	Birth of son, Kermit Roosevelt, at Sagamore Hill
1891	August 13	Birth of daughter, Ethel Carow Roosevelt, at Sagamore Hill
1894	April 10	Birth of son, Archibald Bulloch Roosevelt, in Washington, D.C.
1895	May	Appointed president of the Police Commission of the City of New York
1897	April 19	Appointed assistant secretary of the navy by President William McKinley
	November 19	Birth of son, Quentin Roosevelt, in Washington, D.C.
1898	May 6	Resigns from Navy Department to serve as lieutenant colonel of the First U.S. Volunteer Cavalry Regiment, known as the Rough Riders; travels to Cuba to fight in the Spanish-American War and becomes a hero for leading his troops to victory in the Battle of the San Juan Heights (July 1); promoted to colonel
	September 27	Nominated by Republican Party for governor of New York
	November 8	Elected governor of New York
1900	June 21	Nominated as President William McKinley's vice presidential running mate at Republican National Convention
	November 6	Elected vice president of the United States
1901	March 4	Takes office as vice president
	September 14	McKinley dies as result of assassination attempt; Theodore Roosevelt, age 42, sworn in as president, the youngest man ever to hold the office

1904	June 23	Nominated for president by Republican Party
	November 8	Elected president over Democrat Alton Brooks Parker, with the widest popular margin ever
1905	March 4	Inaugurated president of the United States
1906	December 10	Awarded Nobel Peace Prize for mediating peace in Russo-Japanese War
1909	March 4	Retires from presidency, succeeded by William Howard Taft
	March 23	Sails for Africa with his son Kermit for a hunting trip, followed by visits to heads of state in Europe
1910	June 18	Returns to New York
1912	June	Loses nomination for president at Republican convention
	August	Nominated as presidential candidate by Progressive (Bull Moose) Party
	November 5	Defeated as president by Democrat Woodrow Wilson in three-way race with Wilson and Taft
1914	February 27– April 27	With son Kermit joins expedition for exploration of Brazil's uncharted River of Doubt
1919	January 6	Dies in his sleep at Sagamore Hill

Index

Note: Page numbers in **bold** type refer to illustrations.